M000017438

# EVENTS SPARK CHANGE

---

## A Guide to Designing Powerful and Engaging Events

---

Jennifer D. Collins, CMP

Crescendo
PUBLISHING

To Judge Herald,
May all the events
in your life spark
Positive change!
Best wishes,
Jennifer
10/2018

Events Spark Change: A Guide to Designing Powerful and Engaging Events
By Jennifer D. Collins, CMP

Copyright © 2018 by Jennifer D. Collins

All rights reserved. No part of this publication may be reproduced, distributed, or transmitted in any form or by any means, including photocopying, recording, or other electronic or mechanical methods, or by any information storage and retrieval system, without the prior written permission of the publisher and author, except in the case of brief quotations embodied in critical reviews and certain other non-commercial uses permitted by copyright law.

Crescendo Publishing, LLC
2-558 Upper Gage Ave., Ste. 246
Hamilton, ON L8V 4J6
Canada

GetPublished@CrescendoPublishing.com
1-877-575-8814

ISBN: 978-1-948719-02-5 (p)

ISBN: 978-1-948719-03-2 (e)

Printed in the United States of America

10 9 8 7 6 5 4 3 2 1

# A Message from the Author

Click on the link below the image to hear a special message from Jennifer.

https://youtu.be/NnEEhnORHww

As a bonus gift, I am offering some great resources and tools that will help you start the event design process.

You can download these items by visiting:
www.jdc-events.com

# Table of Contents

# Dedication

I would like to dedicate this book to two major forces in my life. First, to my family, including my parents, W.E. and Evelyn Collins, and my sisters, Stephanie Hammond and Andrea Springer. You've been at the forefront of my every achievement, and I want to thank you for never being at a loss for believing in me, and offering your encouragement and prayers along the way. Nothing I have accomplished could have been done without you.

Second, to Professor Richard Stack, whom I first met in my sophomore year at The American University. You first taught me the principles of public relations, but since then have given me a lifetime of encouragement and generous, thoughtful counsel. For many years, you've been a steadfast advocate for this book, and I want to thank you for your friendship and the positive influence you've had over my life.

# Preface

People often ask me how I got into the event planning industry. It's seemingly a good question, since it really wasn't a fully established "industry" when I first started planning events in the early '90s. Some people wonder why someone would want to juggle so many things that can all come crashing down at the same time. I totally understand that...but I love it.

My entrance into the event management world started around the time I was in college. I am originally from a small town outside of Boston, Massachusetts, and I went to school at The American University in Washington, D.C. While in school, I began planning my family reunion gatherings. I worked with a committee to manage details like scouting for hotel locations and room block arrangements, preparing communications materials, signing contracts, securing food and beverages, coordinating tours, and preparing the agenda/flow and onsite execution. While hosting reunions in such locations as Boston, Washington, D.C., Philadelphia, and Williamsburg, I left no stone unturned in handling all the details.

Given I was carrying a full semester load of classes while planning some of the reunions—and then eventually graduating to full-time employment—I learned the art of multitasking and time management. There was always something to plan and do. But I was good at it, and was known to live my life by lists (and still do).

But even with all the orchestration, the most memorable and exciting part of the process was the end. And not for the reasons you might think, if you've concluded that it was because the exhausting parts were over. It was seeing the smiles on my family's faces. There were so many moments where people were warm in their interactions and engagements. The time spent enjoying the togetherness in sharing a common lineage and experience was palatable. It was that result that solidified my purpose.

I knew that I wanted to create more of those types of experiences, which indirectly led to my desire to start my own business. However, I was still in college at the time and had no idea what type of business to start, even though I knew I enjoyed planning events. So, after graduation, I worked for several Washington, D.C.-based public relations firms, where I pitched stories to reporters and generated coverage of various client programs. From fire safety to infant mortality, to disability education...public education programs and building select conferences and events were my world.

It was a stint at the former National SAFE KIDS Campaign (now SAFE KIDS Worldwide) where I got even more involved with managing community events centered around preventable childhood injuries. In my role as a senior publicist, I supported coalitions across the country with developing press materials to honor National SAFE KIDS Week, and provided logistical support for their local events. The issue of childhood safety was engaging. I enjoyed working with reporters and the SAFE KIDS coalitions to educate audiences about preventable childhood injuries. But what also stuck with me was the power of events to deliver critical information and change behavior. Being able to manage event programs in my full-time work gave me hope and inspiration. It showed me that perhaps I could consider planning events as my own business. If the companies

I worked for could incorporate them into their service offerings, why couldn't I? So I did.

First, as an alumna of The American University, I was fortunate to be able to take classes for "audit" for just $100. I decided to audit a class in the Kogod School of Business, called Entrepreneurship and New Venture Management. This class taught me the principles of starting and running a business. The main feature of the class was the development of a business plan, where we were paired with a teammate to build the plan and deliver a presentation at semester's end. Since I had a venture already in mind, my teammate agreed to use my event planning company as our class project. After we completed the semester and delivered the presentation, I now had my business plan to start my business.

As part of this preparation, I ventured over to George Washington University and took advantage of its free legal clinic. The clinic helped me establish the right type of organization. On November 21, 1997, I went downtown to the Department of Consumer and Regulatory Affairs with my $100 check in hand, and established The Event Planning Group, LLC, which has since been rebranded as JDC Events, LLC. I did this just a few years out of college, while still living in my same basement apartment in the Friendship Heights area of Washington, D.C. My apartment became the company headquarters, and I ran the business on a part-time basis—since I was still working full-time.

I originally chose the company name so people would be clear on what we did. My focus of events was "everything," including corporate and social gatherings such as weddings, birthday celebrations, family reunions, and the like. I soon learned, however, that it was hard to run a business part-time, and I didn't much care for social events. The few weddings I worked on showed me I wasn't as enamored of managing those types of details. I guess it was the emotion of it all—from the bride to the parents, and everything in between. While I still had the desire to create a meaningful experience, I just couldn't get past the process.

During this time, I decided to visit SCORE, a nonprofit association offering advisors and mentors to aspiring entrepreneurs and business owners. I sought SCORE to specifically assist me with marketing. I developed a brochure of my services and target markets, which included social, corporate, and nonprofits. After review, my advisor thought I was trying to be all things to all people. He concluded that those targets had so many different types of events that I should consider narrowing my scope even further. It was good feedback, and also confirmed my desire to move away from social events, instead focusing specifically on the nonprofit, corporate, and government sectors.

My last social event was a 60th birthday celebration for a dear family friend. My friend, Marian, was a renowned educator at Howard University, and she decided she wanted to invite all her friends to celebrate this milestone with her in Jamaica—but at their expense. So she secured my assistance to arrange an all-inclusive package for the hotel, flight arrangements, amenities, and activities. This group was quite challenging, since these were women with very strong opinions.

While I didn't know it at the time, this crew prepared me well for managing strong-willed clients in the future. The event hosted approximately thirty women. We stayed at the Half Moon Resort in Montego Bay, Jamaica. With the assistance of my sister, I orchestrated tours, dinners, and special touches. Marian had a very eclectic group of friends, and she wanted them to get to know each other. So we had assigned seating at different meal functions and provided other opportunities for guests to mix and mingle. Marian remarked all throughout our time away how perfect the seating arrangements ended up. Select members of the group also wanted to share a special birthday greeting from friends not in attendance, whom Marian vacationed with each year on Martha's Vineyard. We made arrangements for the video to be shown after dinner, and orchestrated a cake to be delivered thereafter with candles. As she went to blow out her candles, Marian commented that this experience was everything she had wanted. This was just further confirmation that I wanted to continue creating these type of experiences, though not on a social level. But I would always remember this special event as one that made a difference in someone's life.

After this event, I pulled back on managing any other projects, since it was increasingly difficult to do so part-time. I continued as a senior executive in my current PR firm until I was presented with an interesting opportunity. A friend contacted me and mentioned that the former president/CEO of Choice Hotels was transitioning to a new role as the CEO of the nation's largest nursing home chain. He was looking for an event management company to manage a sales incentive event.

I was intrigued. I was also still waiting for an opportunity to launch myself full-time into managing JDC Events. I was put in contact with the CEO, and we had a great exchange. The event was to celebrate the chain's sales team members, because they'd just had an exceptional year. The chain was looking to host the event in a location such as Scottsdale, Arizona, at a resort with golfing and other amenities.

I prepared a proposal for him, and he approved it. This was in the summer of 2001, and the event was to take place around winter 2001 or early 2002. I felt this opportunity was just what I needed to finally cut ties with my full-time job and build JDC Events. So I ended up quitting my PR firm job around mid-late August of 2001. I alarmed some family members, of course, but felt it was time to "fish or cut bait." After all, and if needed, I assumed I could always find another job.

As we entered into September 2001, plans were in the beginning stages of developing the sales incentive event. I was even making plans to fly out to Ft. Smith, Arkansas, to meet with the CEO of the company to discuss it further. However, the world changed on September 11, 2001, when the United States was hit with the worst terrorist attack in our nation's history. The attack took place two weeks after I had resigned from my full-time position.

Needless to say, everything changed after September 11, 2001. It wasn't quite clear how things would change, but I knew they would. I was scheduled to fly to Ft. Smith, Arkansas to meet with my client on September 13 after the travel ban was lifted. I ended up making the trip, and will never forget the eerie feeling being in Baltimore-Washington International Thurgood Marshall Airport. There was silence and emptiness in the airport. There were only a handful of us on the plane traveling. Change was indeed here.

I arrived in Ft. Smith, Arkansas, and met with the president and CEO of my client company. We had a great meeting and, of course, discussed the news of the day—but not under the impression that it would impact the event. As I returned home and continued forward with contacting resorts in Arizona, the fallout of the terrorist attacks continued. This included people being afraid to travel, meetings being canceled, the economy taking a major hit, and continuing uncertainty. Not long after that, my client decided to cancel the sales incentive event—indefinitely. He didn't feel right celebrating after the country had endured such a traumatic experience.

I totally understood the decision, since that was the position of many organizations during that time. The hospitality industry was hit particularly hard after September 11. Many organizations stopped holding meetings because of the fear of airplane travel. I definitely understood, since it was hard to imagine that such evil could exist. But that didn't mean I wasn't disappointed. That had been my one and only client, and just the push I'd thought I needed to leave my full-time job. The one silver lining, though, was that the client had paid some of my fees—which was helpful in the short term.

What did that mean for JDC Events? It meant I needed to find clients in a severely fractured industry. To keep some funds coming in, I decided to begin substitute teaching, and found an event planning company that hired temporary consultants for on-site management of pharmaceutical programs. This occurred in early-mid 2002, and I then decided to move to Atlanta that summer, thinking it was time to start over somewhere else.

In the midst of all this—and I didn't entirely know it—I was also undergoing a bit of a spiritual transformation. This was not because of September 11; it was something that had occurred in me for years. I felt an emptiness and desire to develop a stronger spiritual foundation. It just so happened to make itself known to me during this time of great uncertainty of how I would survive. In the summer of 2002, I became a born-again Christian. I'd been born and raised in the church, but this experience taught me more about a relationship with God, and it changed my life for the better. The details of that are for another book! But it was indeed a defining moment that totally changed the course of my company and overall way of living. From there forward, I sought guidance and wisdom for my role in this life to make a difference in others' lives. My newfound spirituality also led to a positive transformation in the direction of my business.

During this summer, I looked for projects and began to think I would ultimately close JDC Events, since it was still slow going. However, opportunities began to present themselves—but they were all back in the Washington, D.C., area. I didn't want to move back to D.C., though, so I continued living in Atlanta. Then, another opportunity arrived. It was event-focused, and seemed like a unique project. It was August 2002, and we were approaching the one-year anniversary of the September 11 terrorist attacks. As a response to the attacks, the Transportation Security Administration (TSA) was established to protect the traveling public inside and connecting to the United States. As part of the TSA, security screeners would be commissioned at all airports, and this change was mandated to take effect in the fall of 2002.

In order to meet this goal, there was a search for meeting and event planners nationwide to support a federal contract to screen, train, and hire the security screeners. I was one of the subcontractors hired to assist with managing the training centers, and was stationed in South Bend, Indiana, for approximately two months. During that time, I also assisted training centers in Jackson, Mississippi. My primary role was to coordinate and manage logistics for hotel spaces and conference rooms, arrange food and beverage, and serve as the liaison between hotels and other vendors. We also coordinated swearing-in ceremonies for the new hires. This project was executed Monday through Sunday, as the goal of the contract was to hire approximately 60,000 screeners in a short period of time.

While there was some post-scrutiny of the overall management of the contract, this ended up being a transformational role in the history of our country. Many Americans may not remember a time before we had TSA agents in the airports. So this role was pivotal in my conviction that meetings and events can change society. Some often think that an event is a big, flashy affair with bright lights, music, performers, and other special effects. While that may be true in some cases, it's definitely the exception rather than the rule. And it's also important to note that bigger isn't always better. Many of the meetings and events I planned early on were not large at all. But their focus often sparked some form of change in the people who attended. Whether it is training, learning a new idea, building demand for a product or service, or strengthening stakeholder relationships, the power of any type of event to provoke change is real.

In writing this book, I thought it was important to highlight the origins of JDC Events as it related to purpose. In moving away from social events, it was important for me to build programs that provided results, as opposed to focusing on what some might consider to be glitz and glamor. Why is the event being built? What will it accomplish? What type of change is being sought? Can an event really make a difference? Those and other topics are the types of discussions we'll explore in the coming chapters. Events are powerful forms of communication, and building them wisely can yield memorable and, in many instances, life-changing results.

Many of the events I've built may not be known by their brand, but their impact is powerful. We'll explore some of these examples as well while building a case for managing such programs on your own. Bringing people together is one of the greatest ways to advance as a society and experience positive change. But it's more than just finding a space and inviting people to attend.

Engagement is what enables conference goers to willingly contribute to meaningful outcomes. Having a seat at the table and buying into the process can be the difference between finding a solution or maintaining the status quo. It's the moments created that can be the catalyst to engage and inspire.

After reading this book, I hope you will rethink every event that you've attended or plan to attend in the future. This, specifically in the context of what you walk away with, connections made, and engagement experienced. What nugget of information learned or idea generated can be used to pay it forward? And could you build such an event to speak to your mission and inspire others? It's definitely possible. Any organization, company, community center, church, synagogue, or other entity can build change-making events. Planning and preparation are key, along with a dose of inspiration, resources, commitment, and dedication. There's so much to be accomplished through events, and I hope you'll develop a similar amount of admiration for their power to change lives—and ultimately the world.

# Chapter 1

# Can an Event Really Spark Change?

When people learn of my business, I am often asked, "What's the largest event that you've ever planned." I totally understand the premise of the question, and realize the questioner is intrigued by the prospect. But I still look at that question differently because it suggests that bigger is better. Now, I know that isn't true, but that's simply how it hits me. The other question I get is, "What's your most memorable event?" I really like that question, because it presents the opportunity to explain the most meaningful programs, rather than those determined by size.

There is wonderful power in events. Just think of the positive events you have attended, and reflect on their impact in your life. Did you learn something new? Did you meet someone that changed the course of your business or personal life? How were you able to better yourself after attending the event? According to Merriam-Webster's Dictionary, the definition of an event is "something that happens; occurrence; a noteworthy happening." This means that the entire premise of an event is to make an impact.

As a member of several meeting and event industry organizations, I receive tons of educational publications. As I read through the January 2017 edition of the *Professional Convention Management Association (PCMA) Convene* magazine, I learned of an article that appeared in *Fast Company* in December 2016. This article reports on a man who reduced homelessness in Utah by 91%. According to the article, which summarizes his TEDMED 2016 talk, there are 500,000 homeless individuals in the United States.

The man credited with the reduction is Lloyd Pendleton, who mentioned he had pre-conceived notions about homeless people. He became aware of a new approach to addressing the issue of homelessness called the "Harm-reduction model," which focused on minimizing the negative effects of substance abuse through negotiation and treating the homeless with dignity and respect. However, Pendleton's views changed when he learned of another concept called "Housing First," which focused on providing the homeless with permanent housing as quickly as possible.

So, how did Pendleton learn of this new concept? Through a conference he attended in 2003. This conference discussed the Housing First initiative and its positive outcomes. Pendleton then decided to take what he'd learned from the conference and apply it to his home state of Utah. What was the overall result? According to the article, by 2015, Utah reported that it had reduced its chronic homeless population by 91%—down from 2,000 people to fewer than 200.

A challenging societal problem was successfully addressed due to the vehicle of a conference. And the PCMA article also fittingly pointed out that this remarkable story came to *Fast Company* because of another conference: TEDMED.

When I first read the PCMA and *Fast Company* articles, they just made me smile. They totally demonstrated the power of events. Earlier, you'll remember I mentioned how people ask me about the size of events—but I'd rather answer what events are most memorable instead. This example is the very reason why I love this focus, because it shows an event's ability to change the world one community at a time.

You might wonder if organizations really think along those lines when planning an event. In my experience working on behalf of select organizations, some do and some don't. It depends greatly on the culture of the organization. I have worked with some groups that have not had the mindset to do anything different with their annual events, regardless of whether they've made money or suffered a loss. As we'll discuss in future chapters, building an impactful, change-agent event starts with a mission and purpose. A key question to answer is, what do you want people to do after the event? Identifying the "call to action" is what will set your event on stronger footing to deliver.

I had the unique opportunity to work with the University of California Davis (UC Davis), which had a partnership with the Mars, Incorporated, company. UC Davis is one the nation's top public research universities and a leader in agricultural studies. Founded in 1911, Mars, Incorporated, is one of the largest food companies in the world. Most known for its chocolate such as M&M's and Snickers, Mars has other business divisions such as Petcare, Food, Wrigley, Drinks, and Symbioscience.

The UC Davis and Mars partnership spans decades and is based on cocoa science and other research. Recent advances have been made in understanding cocoa's impact on society in the context of culture and potentially the environment, modern health, and medicine. Both UC Davis and Mars sought to explore and heighten this research in the format of a first-ever Cocoa Symposium. My role was to build the symposium to deliver this objective.

The symposium's purpose was to provide attendees with a series of multi-disciplinary presentations discussing the groundbreaking advances in cocoa research. The goals of the symposium were determined to be threefold:

1. To explore in depth the ability of agriculture to deliver life-changing advances in medicine, nutrition, and public health;

2. To identify and reveal recent scientific advances in cocoa, illustrating its potential ability to positively impact health, nutrition, culture, medicine, and the environment; and

3. To promote and build scientific collaborations to further enhance the positive impact of cocoa and other food crops on society.

Building such an event would be somewhat complex, given the potential for some to discredit the science and the many different organizations needed to bolster the program. The planning began with identifying affiliated organizations conducting various cocoa research projects. This outreach was performed to ensure a broad discussion of cocoa's impact in many different areas. Such partners included the United States Department of Agriculture (USDA), Agricultural Research Service; University of California, Santa Cruz; USDA Forest Service International Programs;

Union of German Academies of Sciences and Humanities; The Royal Botanic Gardens, Kew; Smithsonian Tropical Research Institute; United States Agency for International Development; Chinese Academy of Sciences; World Agroforestry Centre; and the Sustainable Tree Crops Program/International Institute of Tropical Agriculture.

All of these organizations conducted their own cocoa research and were leaders in the industry. It was important to have their voices in the discussion to provide further context and exploration of the crop. Another important aspect was identification of the venue. Given the symposium was the first of its kind, we wanted to choose a venue that had special significance to the topic and was renowned in the field of science. We chose the National Academy of Sciences in Washington D.C., to accomplish this goal. Not only did the venue provide topical stature, but the architecture and environment were beautiful.

Every detail of building such an event was carefully scrutinized and dissected. You might wonder why we focused on these types of details and what they had to do with causing change. The delivery of information is more than just finding any old space and placing a speaker at the front of the room. It's important to spend time building the content and the space for people to best interact, engage, and be receptive to the information. Keep in mind, your "call to action" of the event should always be on the top of your list. In this instance, the goals were to build collaborations and deliver groundbreaking research that would create demand for the information and promote the crop as a potential change-agent. So every part of the symposium's interactions needed to support this focus.

With partners and venues determined, we moved forward with the creation of a theme, agenda, and final presenters.

The chosen theme was "Theobroma Cacao: Ancient Crop, Medicinal Plant, Surprising Future." "Theobroma cacao" is derived from the Greek meaning "food of the gods." The scientific themes of the symposium were determined as plant science of cocoa, anthropology of cocoa, and biomedical implications of cocoa, and presenters were chosen within these disciplines. Of special note is that the date of the symposium was chosen to fall close to Valentine's Day, to supply the "chocolate" hook for the media. Given some of the presentations would focus on the potential heart-health aspects of dark chocolate, there would be deeper explorations of this concept with an additional feature of chocolate tastings throughout the event.

A special part of the symposium was a press conference to announce the groundbreaking findings. The press event was positioned to coincide with the lunch hour so that it wouldn't conflict with the main presentations of the day. Collateral pieces and the event website were developed to communicate to the sponsors, supporters, attendees, and the media. We also wrote a backgrounder to dive deeper into the intent, capture the science of the conference, and promote cocoa's importance in the world. The following is an excerpt from this piece:

"The science of cocoa has recently grown from one of practical application based on empirical observations to one of fundamental understanding based on world-class scholarship integrating state of the art methodologies from diverse disciplines. Recent advances have been made in understanding the value of cocoa to society in the context of culture, the agricultural and environmental potential of cocoa, as well as modern health and medicine. In some ways, it can be viewed as a model for studying the diverse impacts that a unique food crop can have on society at many different levels."

Because this event was a new concept and we wanted to make it easy for people to attend, there was no charge except for personal travel and lodging. While a "free" event could have indicated a lower value, the steering committee realized the credibility and value would be found in the intended scientific presentations, venue, and affiliated organizations. The symposium hosted more than 200 researchers, academics, non-governmental organizations, embassy staff, industry representatives, and government officials. Additionally, there was widespread media coverage of the released research that suggested flavanol-rich foods, such as specific cocoas, could provide an unexpectedly large benefit in the management of the two most common causes of death in today's world: cardiovascular disease and cancer.

An additional benchmark of the symposium's effectiveness was the establishment of the event occurring every two years, expanding to two days and featuring more in-depth discussions on cocoa-related aspects of plant and biomedical science, sustainable agriculture, nutrition, medicine, and anthropology—along with roundtable discussions on issues facing the cocoa- growing regions of West Africa, East Asia, and the Americas.

You'll remember that the goals of the symposium were:

- To explore in depth the ability of agriculture to deliver life-changing advances in medicine, nutrition, and public health;

- To identify and reveal recent scientific advances in cocoa, illustrating its potential ability to positively impact health, nutrition, culture, medicine, and the environment; and

- To promote and build scientific collaborations to further enhance the positive impact of cocoa and other food crops on society.

The power of the symposium was that it introduced and heightened cocoa research and revealed the potential health impacts of the cocoa crop. Prior to this type of symposium, there was no forum for this community to engage on a multi-disciplinary level. The symposium changed the conversation of cocoa science, and took the discussion of the crop to another level. It also positioned the UC Davis/ Mars partnership as an industry leader on this topic.

I mentioned that the success of the first symposium birthed additional symposiums that I also managed. The second one took place again at the National Academies in Washington, D.C. Two years after that, the symposium went on the road to Ghana, West Africa. This location was chosen due to its strength in production, quality, and sustainability practices. It also offered the opportunity for participants to visit a cocoa farm. The results of the third symposium were also impactful, making its planning details especially interesting.

I worked with a select steering committee on the initial details, which included travel to Accra, Ghana, and a presentation to a former Finance and Economic Planning Minister who is now deceased. In Ghana, cocoa is king, with the production accounting for approximately 70% of the world's cocoa beans. Because of this, it was important for us to introduce the symposium to the Ghanaian government, obtain the government's guidance, and secure participation of African scientists to best reflect the region and crop. This meeting was the beginning of that phase, and opened doors throughout the planning of the event to ensure African influence and participation.

Upon the conclusion of the meeting, about a day or so later, the rest of the team departed. That left just me to finish the site visits to various venues in Accra and beyond. I was a guest of the Ghana Cocoa Board, which provided personal transportation support in moving about the region. I must say, it was a nice trip in having the personal attention to support my every move. While I spent time in Accra looking at potential venues, we also traveled about four hours to the city of Kumasi, located in the Ashanti region of Ghana, and one of the largest metropolitan areas in Ghana. I visited another hotel there, and then we headed toward Cape Coast, which was once the largest slave-trading center in West Africa.

When my work was done, I wanted to take the time to see some of the sights of the country, and this was moving and memorable. The day I visited was so lovely. It was quite warm, and the palm trees were gently swaying in the breeze. But I couldn't ignore the past horrors of the castle, where slaves were herded like cattle onto enormous ships, undoubtedly altering the lives of generations to come. I was thankful to have had the opportunity to visit.

As my time in Ghana came to an end, it was undeniably the start of what would be another successful event that had tremendous impact. From the top levels of the Ghanaian government to academia, to researchers and other sectors, the event was built to feature the best research, provide an opportunity to visit the crop, and leave a lasting impact in cocoa-growing regions around the world.

These goals came to fruition as 250 delegates from 14 West and Central African countries, along with cocoa industry leaders, finalized a first-ever sustainable cocoa farming plan for Africa. It was endorsed by Ghanaian President John Agyekum Kufuor, finance, agriculture, and commerce ministers from 14 African nations, scientists, farmers, NGO donor organizations, and other experts. The plan was designed to help cocoa farmers considerably increase their income by growing trees that are higher quality, have more resistance to disease and drought, and consume fewer natural resources.

Events do indeed spark change. Without the Africa-based Cocoa Symposium, and the symposiums leading up to it, this type of result would not have happened. I understand that the prospect of building an event can be intimidating for some. There are so many different moving parts and details that need to be considered. That's why it's critical to have someone in the planning process who can offer expertise and insight on what to expect. But if that's not possible, we'll explore some of the foundational concepts on building transformational events in the remaining chapters. The goal is to spur your thought process on goals and objectives, types of event vehicles to consider, communications, partnerships, and the overall event-building process. It is indeed a puzzle that, when carefully assembled, can yield amazing results.

Creating a memorable event isn't always easy, but it's worth it. It can also yield such power in the lives of those who participate. So, where do you start? Answer the question of what you want to accomplish. Your answer should be more than just, "It would be something *fun* to do." Think about the people who will come to your event. What do you want them to know, do different, or learn? An event without a mission or strong purpose is more susceptible to failure. By spending a considerable amount of time defining your mission, you will be in a better position to roll out a successful program. When exploring further, you should be prepared to spend time in reflection and discussion. It is also important to solicit the right "voices" or opinions that can provide insightful knowledge and perspectives.

In the next chapter, we'll do a deeper dive into the components of identifying the purpose and goals of your event. Think back to the case studies mentioned earlier in this chapter. The first reflected on an individual using an idea he learned to improve the rate of homelessness in his state. The second revealed how a strategic symposium created demand for research that would change the agricultural production of a prized crop. Neither of these events happened overnight, and there was considerable groundwork that went into building a successful outcome.

That's one of the main goals of this book—to help you forge new paths and use events to create change in your world. It doesn't have to be big, or a story that appears on the national news. It's about empowerment to use your tools and resources to deliver a message that's important to you. Never underestimate the power of an event. There is no other part of the marketing matrix as effective as being face-to-face with your intended audience. Now, let's get started looking at the components of building an impactful event—starting with the overall purpose and goals.

# Chapter 2

# What's Your Purpose?

You'll be surprised at the number of people who build meetings and events without a clear mission or purpose. But to ensure your event achieves your goals, you need to put forth a considerable amount of time during this phase. Consider the example of UC Davis and Mars, Inc., mentioned in the last chapter. The purpose of developing the Cocoa Symposium was to educate stakeholders about the recent scientific advances and discoveries in cocoa science. The goals were threefold:

- To explore in depth the ability of agriculture to deliver life-changing advances in medicine, nutrition, and public health;

- To identify and reveal recent scientific advances in cocoa, illustrating its potential ability to positively impact health, nutrition, culture, medicine, and the environment; and

- To promote and build scientific collaborations to further enhance the positive impact of cocoa and other food crops on society.

Every detail and element building the program should then speak to that mission. This helps you stay on target throughout the planning process. Setting a purpose also helps avoid wasting resources. For instance, I know of events that have used the prior year's budget to plan for the next year. While a prior year's budget can serve as a baseline, other major factors need to be considered—especially if you move the event to a more expensive location. In this case, you most likely won't be able to achieve your objectives, because the costs will end up outweighing the details.

When you begin the process, avoid focusing on the tactical elements such as group size, venue, location, and types of presenters. Instead, think strategically about the bigger picture. This focus can be similar to the elements of "human-centered design," which, according to Wikipedia, is a "creative approach to interactive systems development that aims to make systems usable and useful by focusing on the users, designing around their needs and requirements at all stages."

Human-centered design can take time and effort to develop. However, it's the overall concept of thinking more about the user experience that should be your focus. Essentially, where is it that you want to be versus where you are now? If your company is an organization seeking to reduce opioid abuse among targeted populations, your event purpose might be to educate at-risk audiences and industries about the problem to reduce its impact by a certain percentage. Since your objectives are your roadmap, they should be written in detail, measuring the tangible results your event will produce.

Now, understanding that may be all well and good, but there's a reason goal-setting is often overlooked. It's because it's hard. There are often many different people and layers in the overall process. Bringing these elements together can sometimes clog the system and prevent consensus. This process can also be very time consuming. But the more time you spend in this phase, the more focused and better your event will be.

Here's a plan of action to help you start the process:

## 1. Talk It Through

Bring together the key people who have a stake in the overall outcome and success of the meeting or event. Begin by asking such questions as:

- What are you hoping to achieve?
- Who are your key target audiences?
- What has worked well in past events?
- In a perfect world, what would you be able to achieve with this meeting or event?
- How will you measure your success?
- Do you have the human capital and financial resources to support the event?
- What ways do you envision participants engaging in the process?
- What action(s) do you want your audience to take?
- If someone was asked to recommend this event, what would you want them to say?

These are by no means the only questions to ask. Once you begin the process, you'll discover many more. The key is to begin and see where it leads you. This process will help you define your overall event mission statement, which will guide everything you do. It will also offer a closer look at the overall values that will ultimately drive your success.

## 2. Create a Mission Statement

You might question the need for a mission statement. But think about it: if you're interested in meeting a specific goal, a mission statement can be the driver in ensuring that goal is met. According to Wikipedia, a mission statement is "a statement which is used to communicate the purpose of an organization." By creating a mission statement, you stay on target and save time. Everything you do in planning an event is measured by your overall mission. If you are seeking to plan a meeting or event that has meaning in the lives of those attending, it'll be critical to stay on track to ensure your details translate.

## 3. Keep It Moving

Once you walk through the discovery process, it's important to keep moving. There should be one person designated as the engine to keep meeting notes and documentation of conversations. Otherwise, this process can stall, and nothing is accomplished. The key takeaways of your discovery process should be further defined among a smaller group to arrive at where you want to be.

## 4. Set Specific and Measurable Goals

It'll be important to set specific and measurable goals coming out of your discovery process. Try to avoid general statements like, "I want my event to focus on  homelessness." What does that actually mean? There are many different aspects of homelessness to focus on, such as chronic homelessness, etc. Instead, you might say, "I want my event to discuss strategies to reduce chronic homelessness by 50% in six months." This is more specific, but you still want to make sure that your goal is achievable. There are many different factors that impact homelessness, so to drill down further, you might say, "I want my event to discuss housing solutions that reduce chronic homelessness by 50% in five years."

So, instead of being vague, you now have a much clearer goal that is relevant and more motivating. You may have smaller goals that come out of the larger one, but the key is to make them specific and measurable.

**Now, it's your turn. Think through a meeting or event you might be interested in building. Reflect on the steps to arrive at goals and start out by developing a mission statement.**

**Mission Statement**

_____

_____

_____

_____

**Write three goals:**

1. _____

2. _____

3. _____

## How are the goals specific and measurable?

_____

_____

_____

_____

Now that your mission and goals are defined, you're almost there. This marks the beginning of understanding how to innovate, grow your program, and replicate success. I am often amazed at how many organizations have a breadth of information that they don't tap into to help improve their event. While they might have clearly outlined goals and objectives, sometimes there is no follow-up on their effectiveness.

Think back to the questions you asked during the goal-setting process. Follow-up questions that you can ask include:

- What went well? What could we do better?
- Did the event strategy reach stakeholders and other key audiences as intended?
- What were the results of pre-determined measures of success?
- How were participants engaged in the process?
- Were the human capital and financial resources sufficient?
- In what areas could we be more efficient?
- What actions did the audience take?

Gather answers to these questions by hosting another discovery process that will help populate a post-event debrief report. It's much easier to address aspects like these as you are moving through the process, rather than trying to remember at the very end. Whether a one-day or multi-day program, this includes getting feedback from key stakeholders via focus groups, surveys, follow-up calls, and emails. However, you would be surprised at the number of organizations that do not conduct this type of after-action review. But the information gathered is so important to the continuing success of the event. It also places you in a better position to further refine your goals to make more of an impact.

Keep in mind, you will have a more memorable and effective event if your goals are defined. This includes a few key elements:

• Clearly defined purpose on the front end
• Thoughtful review of practices throughout the planning cycle
• Timely post-event debrief

Once you define your goals, you set yourself up for the next step in the planning process: deciding the type of meeting or event to plan. There are many different options, and if your goal is to create a meaningful program, it'll be important to know the best format to match your overall goals.

# Chapter 3

# Types of Events

**CASE STUDY**

*For many years, my company JDC Events has worked with the Siemens Foundation in building and executing an innovative event established by the Siemens Corporation. At Siemens, technology innovation is what fuels the company's success. This also inspires its continual development of technology-based solutions and products. As a company, however, it recognized that it would take more than just research investments to create sustainability for the future. It would require a pipeline of talented people to bring these solutions to life. This is what led to the establishment of the Siemens Foundation in 1998, with the ambitious goal of raising the bar for Science, Technology, Engineering, and Math (STEM) education. Through this effort, the Siemens Foundation made a commitment to developing the nation's future innovators and influencing people and communities in the U.S. and around the world.*

*Siemens chose to meet this forward-thinking challenge through the development of a scholarship event. The Siemens Competition is the nation's premier science research competition for high school students, encouraging rigorous research, challenging student thinking, and understanding of the value of science, while enlightening their consideration of future careers in STEM. Competing students have a chance to win scholarships ranging from $1,000 to $100,000. According to the Siemens Foundation annual report, as of the foundation's 15th year anniversary, STEM job openings grew three times faster than others in the U.S. over the past decade, and demand continues to grow. Today, many of the young people who participated in the program are studying at some of the country's most renowned colleges and universities, while others are already in the workforce making an impact in the field of STEM.*

In the last chapter, we discussed the importance of developing a purpose for your meeting or event. The Siemens Competition outlined a clear goal, and it chose to meet that purpose through the development of a national scholarship competition event.

People have been producing events for centuries, and all with the intent on meeting some form of an objective. Whether large, small, public, or private, the event type is intimately guided by the overall purpose. According to Meeting Professionals International, the United States meetings industry spends more than $122 billion annually. In the past decade alone, the number and variety of events have multiplied significantly. This in large part is due to the increased number of event professionals managing event programs. In 2014, according to the Bureau of Labor

Statistics, there were approximately 100,000 meeting and event planners in the United States. As the industry continues to grow, it can be expected that the number and types of events produced will as well.

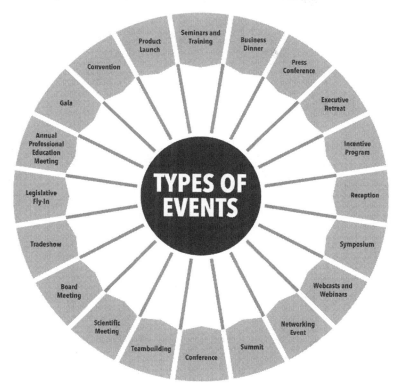

Given that there are so many different types of events, it's critical to understand their purpose so you can achieve your goals. This includes whether you choose to host a live in-person event or virtual program. You might even consider doing a combination of the two in what's often known as a "hybrid" event. Let's explore some of the most common types of events and their overall purposes.

## Live In-Person Events:

### Annual Professional Education Meeting

Whether you are a public relations professional, basket weaver, scrap booker, or skydiver, there is most likely a professional association related to your topic. This type of event is used to provide education and professional development.

### Board Meeting

This type of meeting can be characterized as a gathering of decision-makers for an organization. The meeting addresses the policies and operational aspects of the organization that contribute to its overall functioning.

### Business Dinner

A company or organization promotes this type of gathering for a variety of reasons, including celebrations, discussion of targeted issues, or preparation before a larger event. Depending on the size, this might be done in a restaurant, special event space, or hotel.

### Conference

According to Wikipedia, "a conference is a meeting of people who 'confer' about a topic." Sometimes conference and convention are used interchangeably, but a conference is of shorter duration and designed to meet a specific objective.

### Convention

A convention is a large gathering of people who come together for several days to discuss shared work and other topical interests. These events are usually annual, featuring keynote speakers and other topical presenters.

## Gala
A large gathering that often features dinner and entertainment. It might be used as a fundraiser, celebration, or awards program.

## Incentive Event
An incentive event is a trip used to encourage employees to achieve a specific business goal. This is most commonly used for sales and business development professionals.

## Legislative Fly-In
This type of event is built to educate lawmakers about an organization's legislative priorities. The event is normally a few days, with advocates from the organization making personal visits to legislative representatives on Capitol Hill.

## Networking Event
An event used by professional organizations to bring together members and individuals with common interests for mutual benefit. These can be informal "meet and greets" to more elaborate coordinated events.

## Product Launch
This type of event is used to introduce a new product to the market. Journalists, bloggers, and other media influencers are often invited to the unveiling with the intent of getting them to report on the product's features and use.

## Press Conference
A press conference is used by organizations and newsmakers to make an announcement about an issue or related topic. The press is invited to report on the issue.

## Reception

A reception is a social function used by companies, organizations, and other groups. Receptions are often gatherings that stand alone or precede another event such as a dinner, and often serve light refreshments. They also sometimes feature leaders of the organization delivering short remarks.

## Retreats and Teambuilding

Retreat and teambuilding events bring people together to work as a team toward a common goal. They are usually conducted at an off-site location from a few days to a week.

## Scientific Meeting

This format is where scientists in a certain field come together to learn about advances and new data, along with discussions and networking.

## Summit

A summit is a meeting or conference that features top-level, high-ranking decision-makers to discuss issues of importance to the organization.

## Symposium

Symposiums are meetings featuring subject matter experts who deliver short addresses on a topic or related topics. The presentations discuss trends and recommendations for a specific course of action as it relates to the topic. This format is most often used in academia and the scientific fields, featuring published presenters.

**Seminar and Training**

Seminars and training events are typically shorter events that have a single or multiple speakers leading discussions and training.

**Tradeshow**

A tradeshow is an event where organizations and companies exhibit their products and services to educate and sell to target audiences.

Important factors in deciding on the type of meeting or event format are your overall budget and human capital investment. You'll remember the example of the Siemens Foundation and how it built a scholarship competition to meet its goal of building the next generation workforce in STEM. This didn't come without a cost in terms of the staff and partners who would be engaged to manage the development and production of the program. While there are so many different types of formats to use that can result in an impactful program, your work in the discovery phase will guide the type of event and resources available to produce it.

**<u>Virtual Event</u>:**

With the advancement of technology, virtual meetings and events have become more popular in delivering content via web-enabled computer or tablet. The components of virtual events have also changed over time. There are some virtual events that are built to have the look and feel of a physical environment. For instance, if you have visited a tradeshow floor, some virtual events look just like that with a setting of booths, people, signage, and interactivity. There might be chat rooms and other ways for participants to engage as well. However, virtual events also include webcasts of meetings and events, webinars, and virtual demos.

Virtual events can be used to deliver content such as speaker presentations, trainings, meetings, company-wide gatherings, and other content. The virtual format has allowed companies and organizations to reduce their travel by hosting their meeting online. There are also organizations that create what are called "hybrid" meetings or events, which are a combination of in-person and web events.

In building a virtual event, it's most worthwhile to approach it as if you are building a community. So it's important to include elements where people can connect before, during, and after the event. At the beginning, they may be able to provide their information and topical interests, asking questions during the event and then following up with other participants with similar interests once it concludes. Additionally, while virtual events may remove the cost of travel, most still have equivalent costs to meeting room rental in the form of virtual event software, video cameras, production, and management costs. There is also a need for the appropriate levels of bandwidth from the venue, as well as audio-visual equipment such as microphones for an audio feed. It is important to produce the highest quality virtual event so there is no distraction for the attendee to fully participate in the meeting.

Virtual events are still evolving, and I anticipate that as technology continues to advance, related industry trends and practices will do the same.

# Chapter 4

# Stakeholder Engagement and Communications

## CASE STUDY

*The mission of the First Responder Network Authority (FirstNet) is to develop, build, and operate the nationwide broadband network that equips first responders to save lives and protect communities. FirstNet was established as one of the last recommendations of the National Commission on Terrorist Attacks Upon the United States, or "9-11 Commission." The 9-11 Commission was an independent, bipartisan commission that prepared a full account of the circumstances surrounding the September 11, 2001, terrorist attacks, and how to guard against future ones. FirstNet was authorized by Congress in 2012.*

*My company was contracted by FirstNet to assist with developing six consultation workshops among federal, state, tribal, and local public safety entities to ensure that the FirstNet network would be designed to meet the needs of public safety across the country. The workshops were hosted in strategic locations across the country, designated by regions representing all fifty states and U.S. territories. We also partnered with the National Governors Association Center for Best Practices, so each state's governor could identify the public safety professionals to send to each of the workshops.*

*This process was a large undertaking, since every state would require different needs to support the broadband network. Our team worked with FirstNet to develop the agenda for each workshop, which was created to accommodate sensitive issues that might be discussed. This included identifying the speakers and scope of their presentations, as well as managing the invitation process and overall event logistics. The logistics were time sensitive and complex, in that many of the meetings overlapped since this effort was done in a period of six weeks.*

*From beginning to end, the success of this effort was about engagement and communication—initially to build the working relationship with states and provide the opportunity to listen and work collaboratively within a peer-to-peer setting. The six consultation workshops were essential in creating these working relationships, while learning from the thousands of public safety professionals who would be the stakeholders in the success of building the network. Hearing directly from the people on the ground about their capacity, challenges, wireless assets, and infrastructure was critical to beginning the design of a network.*

*Given the extraordinary level of coordination, the workshops delivered an open and productive process in the exchange of information while sharing the commitment to the first responder community. Without the ability to host the meetings in the designated timeframe and obtain the much-needed information to begin preparing for the network, the mission and goals of the program would not have been accomplished. It was also important that the process engage key stakeholders for their input and participation, while adopting continuous communication practices, so everyone involved was knowledgeable about the intended goals and mission.*

## Why Identify Stakeholders?

The most important reason for identifying stakeholders is that it allows you to engage them as part of the event effort. Not only will you have access to their expertise, but they'll offer a deeper level of credibility and additional resources—whether financial, human capital, or related connections—to produce a stronger event. Some of the other advantages of identifying stakeholders include:

- Expands ideas and perspectives
- Increases credibility of the intended effort
- Generates buy-in and support for the effort—everyone takes ownership
- Exposes potential sensitivities that should be considered
- Strengthens your position
- Builds bridges and connections
- Increases likelihood of success

Working with different stakeholders and groups is a backbone of building successful meetings and events. In many instances, planning by committee is often standard operating procedure. I recently appeared on a panel of communications professionals discussing how to produce strategic events. One of the attendees asked the question of how to work with varying opinions when you're developing events. It was a great question, and one that many event professionals experience when managing event programs. The answer lies in the stakeholders and decision- makers. It's important to know who ultimately will be charged with making the final decision and what their motivation is in relation to the key stakeholders.

So, who exactly *are* stakeholders? There are several, and they are internal and external. Essentially, they are individuals or organizations who have an interest in your activity or may be impacted by your activities—whether positively or negatively. Consider the case study at the beginning of this chapter. The key initial stakeholders for FirstNet were the public safety officials within all fifty states and territories. To define and identify the stakeholders in your event, the first step is to ask probing questions about impacts and outcomes, such as:

- Will they be directly or indirectly affected, and will it be a positive or negative influence?
- Will they have concerns or opinions?
- Do they represent any potential conflicts of interest?
- Are we legally bound to them?
- Will they have a role in the solution?
- Are they currently operating in this space?

As you identify them, you should also consider asking stakeholders for other potential targets, and consult with organizations that have been involved in similar efforts.

When considering stakeholders, internal and external targets might include:

- Leadership and members of an association, company, or organization that are similar in subject matter
- Service suppliers
- Employees, volunteers, and workforce
- Regulatory authorities
- Customers, delegates, visitors
- Exhibitors, speakers, participants, sponsors
- Emergency services, security
- Local community, neighborhoods, and networks

Stakeholders should have a role to play, whether internal or external. For instance, for FirstNet, the role of the public safety professionals was to identify the challenges, sensitivities, and state resources for building the broadband network. Those particular stakeholders were involved in the initial planning phase. Some stakeholders will be involved in managerial planning, and their overall actions might be more internal. When considering stakeholders for events, you might consider categorizing further by asking these questions:

- Are they involved in operational decisions—before, during, or after the event?
- Will they interact with participants and influence their behavior?
- Do they make final decisions on purchases?
- Are they required to perform certain duties related to the event?

Once you have clearly identified the stakeholders and understand the best approaches to engage them, you'll need to plan a communications strategy to exchange information. This might be reaching out to them directly, providing a formal letter of invitation, or having a third party in the process. The key is understanding the best way to capture their attention so you secure successful engagement.

## Stakeholder Communications

Communicating with stakeholders is an important process. They can make or break your event, given your need for their influence and ideas. In the case of FirstNet, the organization hosted consultation workshops to engage its stakeholders. We designed a program to provide a transparent process to share information and build working relationships that would continue throughout the effort.

This was also similar to building the Cocoa Symposiums, where our planning process featured key stakeholders that comprised a steering committee. The success of that project relied on engagement of the stakeholders and a strong communications plan to ensure they were involved. What this means is that you, as the event manager, need to have a firm understanding of what you want from each stakeholder. There are varying reasons why you want them involved, and they too will have their own perspectives. Some may try to dominate the process with their input and suggestions. Others may not be as engaged as you might want them to be. It's the role of the event and project manager to balance the personalities and goals so your event benefits positively from their input.

How do you do this? Through communication and transparency. Once you've defined the stakeholders, you should develop a formal mechanism for them to be involved in the process. This might be through a "steering committee" that has a representative from your stakeholder groups available to participate in scheduled conference calls and meetings. Each steering committee representative speaks on behalf of the representative's organization or company to ensure its voice is included in the process. You should also develop a determined timeframe for meetings. Everyone has competing schedules, and you want to make sure you have the right people in each of the planning meetings. This timing might start out monthly if the event is farther away. You might need more regular meetings for subsets of the steering committee who are working on specific aspects of the event. These might entail a stakeholder tasked with doing a presentation, or marketing materials that need to be developed. Even then, there should be scheduled meeting times for the most effective communication to work toward a successful event.

Keep in mind that, oftentimes, you may not have a relationship with the stakeholder. In these instances, your outreach may need to be more formal. This might include sending a letter of invitation describing the event and conducting a presentation. You'll remember in Chapter 1 where I explained the process of building a Cocoa Symposium in Ghana. During that planning, I delivered a presentation as a member of the planning team to the former Finance and Economic Planning minister of Ghana. He was a critical stakeholder, as we needed the country's buy-in to host the Cocoa Symposium and engage its scientists. Prior to the presentation, we sent a formal letter of correspondence to introduce the symposium and request the meeting.

It's important to keep each stakeholder's expectations and needs in mind throughout each conversation, email, or report—no matter how casual or formal the communication. Remember that your company's or organization's interests are more important than any individual's, which includes yours or a stakeholder's. When forced to choose between them, put your organization's needs first. What I've found is that stakeholders will respect the event manager who displays the following character traits:

- Transparent and honest

- Shares the hard facts

- Listens

- Consistent and reliable

- Takes ownership of the event

- Accountable for mistakes and stands by decisions

Many people don't realize that building events is one large exercise in communication. It's communications between the project organizers, the planning team, and stakeholders—and the event itself is the way these messages are delivered. That's why it's important to spend a lot of time cultivating relationships, building trust, and, most importantly, listening. Sharpening your listening skills will be vital to the success of your event. Events that deliver information to change communities, or brand a company as a leader, or strengthen relationships while creating memorable experiences, don't just happen by chance. The event manager needs to always be listening to achieve such results. There are so many different factors that can disrupt the communication cycle. Some of these could be your client's emotions, your own perceptions, or other external factors.

That's why you have to always be in a position to listen, which will guide your overall thoughts and actions—even if you may not agree with an idea or vision. For instance, I had a client whose company was celebrating a milestone anniversary, and the company decided it did not want a formal event program prior to a dinner. This meant that after the dinner was served, it wanted anyone and everyone to have the opportunity to take the stage to share their thoughts about the company and memorable experiences. While there were several stakeholders identified as part of the event's outreach, one segment included people who had been let go from the company. Some of these individuals were invited to the event, and it was unclear how this would turn out—and whether someone might use the opportunity for retaliation. However, the president and CEO would not budge from this format, even as our team shared the possible ramifications.

Since we could not convince the president and CEO to adopt a more controlled program, we hired plain clothes security personnel to be available in case of any issues. By offering this type of format, the president and CEO hoped to convey a more meaningful and unscripted evening. The goal was for individuals to share more of their hearts with the crowd rather than appearing "staged." We definitely listened and understood the vision, but it didn't mean we were in agreement with it. But I am thankful that nothing sinister occurred that evening. The event resulted in being a positive and stunningly memorable one for all guests.

Achieving a project's objectives takes a focused, well-organized event manager who can engage with a committed team and gain the support of all stakeholders. Building strong, trusting relationships with interested parties from the start can make the difference between project success and failure.

However, as with any type of ongoing initiative, you have to keep at it for as long as the effort lasts. New stakeholders may need to be brought in as time goes on. Old ones may cease to be actual stakeholders, but may retain an interest in the effort and therefore continue to be included. It's critical to maintain stakeholders' motivation, keep them informed, and/or continue to find meaningful work for them to keep them active. Understanding and engaging stakeholders can be tremendously helpful to your effort, but only if it results in their commitment and ownership of their role.

This is why most of your effort in engaging stakeholders needs to start at the identification process. Going back to the beginning of this chapter, we discussed FirstNet and the consultation workshops. The identified public safety stakeholders remain active and engaged in the planning of FirstNet's broadband network. While the six consultation workshops were the initial rollout, there has been continued work since then. The organization continues to engage the original stakeholders, while targeting others, so the mission can continue forward. The engagement includes communications, regular meetings, and events to keep stakeholders active and involved. Nurturing those with a vested interest will ensure the success of your event. With that understanding, you'll be able to invite their involvement, address their concerns, and demonstrate how the effort will benefit them.

Analyzing your stakeholders, which determines their level of interest and influence over the event, can make management easier. Once you complete an analysis, you can then decide on the appropriate approach for each individual and group. Depending on your goals, you may either focus on those with the most interest and influence, or those who are most affected by the event. It's important to remember that you are not able to do it all. Trust others enough to allocate tasks to them.

You can think of engagement and communications as the engine of the event process. This is what starts the wheels turning after the preparatory work of defining goals and objectives, and understanding what type of event to pursue. Engaging and communicating with stakeholders will carry you through the life cycle of the event process. It will transition and morph into other aspects, depending on what situations or details occur at any given time, but it will definitely set a firmer foundation as you build a successful event. You'll just need to make sure to assess the effectiveness of your communication and make adjustments as needed. It's important to remember that this should be a mutually beneficial relationship for both you and the stakeholder.

This may sound like hard work, and in certain instances it can be, but you will be in a much better position to deliver a stronger event if you make the investment wisely. You'll also then be ready to build the rest of your event. Events that are memorable and create change in people's lives are all about deliberate planning. Many of the conversations you have with your stakeholders will not only fuel content, but elements of the logistics as well. That's why it's so important to spend time in this phase identifying what you want from your identified stakeholders. When building the Cocoa Symposium in Washington, D.C., we knew that hosting the event at an esteemed science-based organization would lend additional credibility to the event and further brand the scientific presentations. We determined that the National Academy of Sciences (NAS) would be the best fit, which ended up being a key stakeholder. Not only does NAS provide objective, science-based advice on critical issues affecting the nation, but it boasts the country's leading researchers in science. The NAS building is also one of the most beautiful buildings in the Washington, D.C. area in terms of architecture and scientific elements.

Having access to the NAS bolstered the status of the symposium. It also raised the profile of NAS in featuring its researchers. So how an event is built directly benefits from certain stakeholders. Your event may not exist or do as well without them. As you begin to build your event, the stakeholders should be involved in the process, since their resources, perspectives, and expertise are why you consider them to be stakeholders in the first place. Making them feel heard strengthens the bond of the relationship and creates ownership of contributing toward the event's success.

Whether sourcing the venue, creating the program content and flow, introducing special elements and room setups, or managing catering (among other tasks), your stakeholders can help fine-tune your activities so you can continue to appeal to your target audiences. While you may not adopt every aspect the stakeholders offer, it should be a common practice to obtain their input and incorporate feedback as appropriate.

# Chapter 5

# Designing the Event

## CASE STUDY

*My company produced a conference on behalf of a client representing a membership-based association for microbusiness development. The mission of this organization is to assist underserved entrepreneurs in starting, stabilizing, and expanding businesses. The majority of participants at the conference were financing and technical support organizations that provide services to small businesses. The multiple-day conference would feature a series of keynote presentations and breakouts with the intent of dissecting the major issues related to microbusiness development and sustainability. However, the client was interested in doing more than just planning a conference. The organization wanted to build a program where participants would be actively involved in the event from beginning to end.*

*After considerable discussions about the purpose, goals, success factors, and intended experience, our team honed in on just that—the experience. We knew that the experience would seal the event's stature in the mind of its participants. When the team began planning, we thought through what participants would experience from the time they arrived onsite throughout the duration of the conference. We focused on creating a multisensory event, or an event that speaks to the five senses: sight, sound, smell, taste, and touch.*

*The event took place at a hotel, and our team worked with the client on creating visuals that would launch participants into the mood of the conference. Given the conference focus was small business or "Main Street," we wanted to incorporate that theme into the details. Many of the sessions were scheduled to take place in the main conference room, so we decided to create a "Main Street" backdrop to support the theme. This included building a 3-D stage that featured a hardware store and bakery that had images of people inside the windows. We decorated the stage with lamp posts, real benches, and trees—elements you would see as you walked down Main Street, USA. This visual set the stage for all presentations, whether keynotes or panelists. At different times, some of the speakers even sat on the benches on the stage as they waited for their turn to speak. Many speakers also gestured to being on Main Street during their presentations, which brought everyone into the moment.*

*Additional elements included the smell and taste of select foods during meal functions, the touch of materials that reflected the overall theme, and sounds of music throughout the event. All of these subtle influences were carefully crafted to enhance the messages of the event. They contributed to setting the tone and giving each of the participants an experience. The feedback received reflected this notion, with many participants stating they felt as if they were downtown on Main Street. They also commented that they were re-energized and even more committed to supporting the plight of small businesses.*

There are so many elements that contribute to building a successful event. The opening case study shows how speaking to the five senses can create an impactful and memorable event. Our senses are the foundation of our experiences, yielding rich, immediate, and vivid interactions. The more the senses are stimulated, the more memorable the experience, since they activate the brain. Think about a time when you smelled a familiar scent and suddenly experienced déjà vu. Smell can be one of the most powerful senses because of the memories it produces. According to a study by the Sense of Smell Institute, while people recall only about 50% of visual images after three months, they recall smells with a 65% accuracy after an entire year. The senses stimulate a new way of thinking, and experiences become more memorable when multiple senses are triggered.

Even though smell is the most powerful sense, the most dominant ones used in events are sight and sound. They are the easiest and can often generate the most impact. According to a 2015 survey of event professionals conducted by London and Partners and CWT Meetings & Events, when asked to cite roadblocks to building multisensory experiences, the responses included: limited budgets (43%), lack of time (26%), and inability to find sensory content (24%). One thing that resonates so deeply with me is that bigger is not always better. It's interesting that many of the survey respondents mentioned not having the budget to produce a multisensory event. However, it doesn't have to be all that complex. It should just be meaningful in thought and preparation.

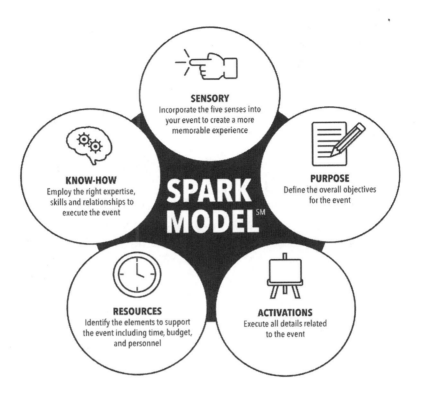

This focus is what serves as the engine in building successful events, and what led me to establish the SPARK Model℠—a five-phase plan for designing meetings and events. The five phases—Sensory, Purpose, Activations, Resources, and Know-How—represent distinct guidelines that move you through the designing process. It's important to remember that the SPARK Model℠ is an approach that individuals can use as a starting point. As you begin to work through the process, there will be other factors that emerge, impacting the overall design. But SPARK can be a starting point, as each element works in tandem with the other.

## Sensory

Sensory is understanding and considering the role and impact of the five senses in building meetings and events. Scientific brain studies confirm that the more a person's senses are stimulated during an experience, the more memorable it becomes, creating greater engagement. Smell can be the most powerful of the senses, which will be discussed later on in the chapter. But event professionals should consider using the senses as a tool to enhance the imagination and experience of event participants.

## Purpose

As discussed in Chapter 2, purpose explores the reasons behind creating the meeting or event. This is one of the phases where you should invest significant time identifying whether an event is the right step—and, if so, what you want to achieve in building one.

## Activations

Building on the purpose, activations are where you begin to set the objectives in motion. This includes building out how you will execute the sensory elements and deliver the experience for your participants.

## Resources

As described in Chapter 6, there are a considerable number of resources to consider when building an event. These include such factors as time, budget and personnel.

## Know-How

This phase represents the right skills, expertise, and relationships to meet your objectives. It should also include evaluation components that can be used for successful design of future programs.

Events have incredible power to spark change, and the method of using the senses to achieve this goal can help drive that change. Since the sensory phase is such an important part of the designing process, it's important to understand the role and impact of each sense in-depth:

## Sight

This is one of the senses that dominates the role in building many meeting and event environments. Just as the staging described in the case study suggested, the sight of the 3-D Main Street transferred guests into the actual environment, creating a memorable effect. Whether it's lighting that's used to emphasize a stage, logos projected on screens or walls, signage with creative designs conveying a message, or creative food displays and presentations, the sight of the event can be one of the most impactful experiences. The key is making sure you speak to your objectives. I've seen many events projecting sensory overload, where it felt like being in New York's Times Square with lights flashing, tons of images projecting, and overall confusion. Delicate, customized, and thoughtful touches that meet the objectives of your event are what resonate with participants. It doesn't have to be many—just carefully crafted to create harmony. When considering sight, you might start with some of the following questions:

- What is the goal of your event?
- Who is your target audience?
- What message do you need to convey?
- What location would be most appropriate for the event?
- Why will they attend?
- Are there any special features or elements that resonate specifically with this audience?

- What types of aspects are appealing to the audience?

There will be plenty more questions that arise once you begin the process. The key is remembering your overall objectives and how they can fuel the sense. For instance, when building events for federal government agencies, hosting them at luxury hotels boasting ornate décor and expensive trimmings wouldn't necessarily be the right venue for their events. The government is focused on spending taxpayer dollars wisely, so it may opt for another hotel that is less extravagant but can still effectively convey its message. In this instance, perhaps there are other sight features that can be created to achieve impact—such as lighting, logo placement, and theme-related signage, among other elements. It's critical to know your audience and what will best translate so it's done with tact and style.

## Sound

Sound can be a powerful sensation. However, don't confuse loud with power. While it's important to hear remarks or music when at an event, you don't want to drown out the event activity. For instance, think about being at a reception where the voice noise level among guests has a volume in and of itself. While many organizers will include music as part of the reception, there are some that end up raising the volume above the voices, causing people to have to yell to hold a conversation. Unfortunately, that detracts from the reception rather than adding to it. When planning the sound design of your event, there are several questions you should address:

- *What is the dominant sense of your event?* Sound might be the dominant element if you are featuring speakers or live performances and music. This will require you to make the investment in high quality sound system production.

- *How will sound help reinforce or expand the guests' interaction with the event?* For instance, at a client's 20th anniversary event, there was a dance floor. The DJ planned for guests to celebrate during a heavy hors d'oeuvres reception. The sound was used as a way to promote celebration and engage guests to dance and have fun.

- *Is the architecture of the venue conducive to optimal sound quality?* There are certain spaces—such as those with a dome ceiling, a sky atrium, or long room—that may not be as inviting for the use of sound. The sound might bounce throughout the room, create echoes, or not extend far enough to the back for guests to hear. I have attended receptions with nearly 1,000 people where speakers were positioned in the front of the room. However, when they delivered their remarks to the crowd, only those in the front could hear them. Those in the back continued to talk and mingle during the reception since the sound didn't travel. So it's your responsibility to do your homework prior to choosing a venue to ensure it will meet your requirements.

## Smell

Earlier, we discussed that smell is the most powerful of the senses because it triggers emotions. The sense of smell, also known as the "olfactory system," is closely linked with memory. Think about elements such as pine or gingerbread; these scents are often associated with Christmas and may conjure up thoughts of childhood as well as the overall season. Or a smell of certain flowers may elicit memories of holidays, special occasions, or another memorable point in time. This can often happen spontaneously, with a smell triggering an immediate memory. While this sense is the most powerful, it's not used as widely within the event industry. Scents can be tricky, in that some scents may not elicit the type of reaction you want. Instead of pleasurable memories, it might evoke just the opposite. This is not something you can necessarily know, as it could be very direct and personal to the individual. Scents are also not widely used due to the potential for allergic reactions. So you'll need to be careful in your application and venture back to what we previously discussed in knowing your audience.

Another factor to consider with scents is the actual venue. When conducting site visits, take note of whether there are unnatural smells like a deodorizer that could be used to cover up other smells. Venues with a natural smell are the best.

**Taste**

When designing for food functions, it's important to speak with the catering team to discuss your goals and objectives for the presentation and how to partner the sense of taste with the other four senses. It should work in tandem with the other senses, not just as something to do. For instance, if your event is on Cape Cod and you decide to feature a coastal New England-style theme, then it wouldn't make sense to serve Italian, Thai, or Mexican foods. Most likely, you would serve good old-fashioned clambake-style fare, fish dishes, clam chowder, and summer cookout selections. As with all the other senses, you should keep your audience in mind. This includes knowing the age, culture, and overall lifestyle of your guests. The taste of the event is one of the most important, and can be equally powerful in transforming guests from spectators to participants who will remember the event you've designed.

## Touch

The sense of touch can be as simple as bag giveaways, linens on a table, a printed program, or a logo cookie, or as engaging as game displays, a cooking class, paint lounge, or audience polling using cell phones. There are many different ways to accomplish touch that can fit the piece of your event puzzle nicely. As with sight, it's important to know your overall goals and what would be appropriate. You also want to be cautious about not going overboard. One of the greatest features of the touch sense is that you can further brand your particular event. Whether it's a handbag, cell phone cover, autographed book, folder of materials, or other item, the touch feature offers the opportunity to not only get involved with the event, but to extend the brand of your company or organization. However, it's important for you to know your target audience and what item would most resonate with them.

As you start thinking through multisensory events, it can be easy to get carried away. So it's definitely a strategy that needs to be managed. Make sure you carefully select those design elements that support the goals and objectives of the event. You'll notice that's a running theme throughout this book. That's also why you should use the SPARK Model$^{\text{SM}}$ as your overall guide.

You don't want to confuse or irritate your participants by layering too much creativity at one time. If you commit to spending more time in the Purpose phase of the SPARK Model$^{\text{SM}}$, you'll be in a better position to think through what you want to achieve.

This strategy is one that can be used in any type of meeting environment—whether a special event, meeting, conference, convention, or any other type of format where people are coming together.

## Activating Your Goals

This—understanding what you want to achieve when developing an event—will be an area where you spend a good amount of time. We've discussed how to use the senses to design an impactful and memorable event. Now, let's pair that knowledge with the nuts and bolts of some of the following event elements:

## *Venue*

Similar to real estate, "location, location, location" is the name of the game when managing events. This decision will be based on your overall purpose and goals, and will need to provide the best features and accommodations for participants to effectively engage with them. For instance, in thinking about the senses and their impact on events, you should consider venues that come with built-in features like high ceilings, greenery, windows, established décor. This will largely depend on the type of event that you are hosting; remember the example cautioning use of a luxury hotel for a government meeting. There are many questions you need to ask before you begin the designing process. Some considerations include:

- *Who is the intended audience?* If you know the demographics of your audience, designing the elements, tone, space considerations, and tempo will be easier to execute.

- *What is the actual event?* While there are many venues that are versatile, it still wouldn't make sense to hold the circus in a downtown business hotel. It's important to know the type of event to make sure the space works best for it.

- *Why is the event being held?* The purpose helps determine what type of venue you will need. Is the purpose to celebrate, network, educate members or employees, or provide professional development?

- *When will the event be held?* Timing is a big consideration, as this can impact cost, availability, and overall options.

- *Where will the event be held?* You'll need to make sure the venue is appropriate for your intended audience. This includes capacity, perception, distance, cost, and overall atmosphere you hope to achieve.

- *Is there a budget?* Event costs can be managed effectively once you identify the details and parameters.

- *How will the event be executed?* Does your organization have the resources to design and host the event? This includes human capital expertise, access to quality vendors, management practices, and established protocols and procedures.

No doubt the answers to these questions may generate more, but they are an essential start to designing the experience that will prove effective for your audience.

### *Event Layout*

Designing the space to suit your audience will rely heavily upon your intended goals. Making it easy for participants to move around and participate in the meeting, while being engaged, can be an art. When developing an overall layout, consider all aspects of your event—from the size and weight of equipment to what you want participants to feel, smell, taste, hear, and see.

## SAMPLE ROOM LAYOUTS

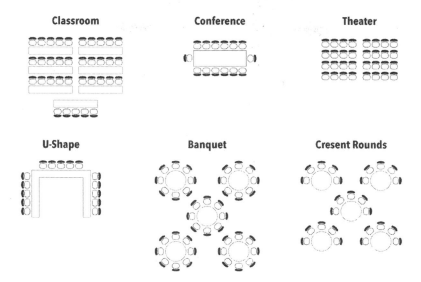

There are standard layouts, such as Theater style, Classroom, Banquet, U-shape, Conference, Crescent Rounds and others. However, knowing your audience can help you think creatively and push the envelope in using alternative space formats. The venue staff can also help you think through such options so your unique format can create a memorable and engaging experience.

### *Speakers/Presenters*

Your content and presentation will be totally driven by the type of event you are designing. For instance, will it be a motivational program, concurrent learning sessions, a networking program, or an anniversary event? Understanding the "why" behind what you're doing will yield the best type of content to deliver your message.

## *Entertainment*

Entertainment is not appropriate for every type of event, but even the sound of music before or between conference sessions could offer memorable depth to your event.

## *Food and Beverage*

You can accomplish so much through food and its presentation. In preparing for meal functions or including food as any part of an event, it's important to understand the participants' expectations. Meal functions are personal, and take time to design. Aspects like budget, location, equipment, space, culture, timing, and presentation are all factors in delivering a successful meal function. Also keep in mind that the sight and taste of the food will play into delivering a memorable experience.

There are so many different dietary requests nowadays from gluten free to vegan to vegetarian—that it's important to discuss these special requests with the catering team. Use the menus provided by the catering team—whether inside the venue or via a caterer—as guides. If you have a certain type of fare and presentation you want to serve, discuss that with the catering staff and chef, and they'll determine what can be done. Take your time in designing the food and beverage service. Open communication and planning ahead are the keys to ensuring presentation and delivery successfully complement your event.

## *Audio-Visual*

Earlier, we discussed the importance of sound in complementing an event. Whether a quartet is playing quietly in a corner or a DJ is blasting tunes with people on the dance floor, the type of music and scope will be determined by the event and overall objectives. You'll also need to work with audio-visual (AV) professionals, who will deliver the sound and overall effects successfully. Consulting with the venue's AV staff—or an outside AV company—is the first step in discussing your overall needs, requirements, and expectations. The AV company is a critical partner in the process, and should be aware of your event details so it can provide the proper context to meet your requirements.

Designing and executing events is a large undertaking with many moving parts. No one person can do it alone. Thinking about building an event that can potentially transform participants' lives takes strategy, time, expertise, and resources. Also keep in mind that this doesn't just pertain to large productions. You have the power to make a difference, whether in a community organization or a 5,000-person conference. The key is having the right resources in place to help you achieve your goals, which will be discussed in the next chapter.

# Chapter 6

# The Right Resources

**CASE STUDY**

*My company is based in the Washington, D.C., area, which can make it unique in the types of events we produce. For instance, there are many organizations, corporations, and associations that are interested in advocating for their issue on Capitol Hill. The events are often called "Legislative Fly-Ins" or "Advocacy Days," and we provide strategy and logistical support to assist with these programs. A client organization that advocates on behalf of charter schools holds an annual Legislative Fly-In that we have managed over the years. This association approached our company due to not having the expertise, personnel, or logistical know-how to bring approximately 100 members of its association to meet with their Congressional members on the Hill. Our team launched into action by preparing a work plan, which included securing a room block at a nearby hotel and coordinating meeting space for an orientation, preparing logistical details to make travel arrangements, coordinating all venue details (including audio-visual arrangements, food and beverage details, staging, and flow), preparing and printing signage and handout materials, coordinating ground shuttles to move members between the hotel and Capitol Hill, and ordering awards as part of the organization's awards program for select members of Congress who were champions for its issue. We also had to execute all details onsite.*

*We provided additional support by confirming appointments with Congressional members before the event, and dispatching our team inside each of the House and Senate Office Buildings to serve as directional guides on the day of the event. In this role, our team worked closely with Congressional staff who served as our point of contact to make last minute changes as needed. This included alerting us to changes in office locations or if a member became delayed at the building's security checkpoint. We had the cell phone numbers of all association members making the visits, and we contacted them to alert them to any changes or direct them if they got lost.*

*Our company worked directly with the vice president of federal advocacy and an assistant who was charged with overseeing the details and scheduling the appointments. The logistical details, expertise in coordination, vendors, appointments, and directions to association members onsite were critical resources that supplemented the organization's capabilities. The results of our efforts included the creation of favorable legislation and the recognition of other organizational priorities. Because we utilized the necessary resources, the organization was able to focus on its core capability.*

We discussed in Chapter 5, the "R" in the SPARK Model<sup>SM</sup> represents Resources. These are critical to building events that are meaningful and effectively meet your objectives. If there isn't enough focus on whether you have the right resources, you most likely won't be successful in your process. Resources can mean many things, including time, budget, human capital, and expertise. There are some organizations that are often deficient in only one of these areas. However, as in the case study, there are others that need multiple resources to pull off an event. As you begin the planning, it'll be important to know what's available to you.

**Time**

Many organizations are interested in hosting an event; however, they want the planning to happen in a short period of time. While there are some events that can be done last minute, it really depends on the type of event and what you're trying to accomplish. If done last minute, there's a good chance your costs may increase, the right target audience may not have time to attend, or you'll have to "make do" with the chosen space or other elements impacted by time. Understandably, a last-minute event is sometimes out of your control. But if you do have a say, a longer lead time is always better.

This will give you time to properly promote the event and plan it so your goals and objectives are thoroughly addressed. It will also help you think through any potential surprises while buying time to build any necessary stakeholder relationships or target certain speakers who will ultimately help strengthen your message and outreach. Something else to consider is whether your event will overlap with any other programs that may target the same audience. For the most effective events, you should seek to have time on your side for the best result.

## Budget

Budget planning for your event can be the difference between holding an event or not. That's why it's important to have open and honest discussions about the budget. This also helps to leverage expectations, as it's simply not possible to want top-of-the-line features and elements if you're not willing to pay for them. Knowing your overall priorities is imperative, since every element of the event will be affected by the budget. For instance, we've worked with organizations that have had large budgets for notable speakers and other potential features that would draw people to the event. Some of these same organizations allowed a very small budget for such aspects as food, beverages, and overall management of the event. The money should be spent on what's considered of value, determined at the very beginning of the designing process. If history exists of your intended event, then at least three years of data would serve as a great starting point in assembling the budget. The budget items might include features like staff labor, space rental, audio-visual, travel, food and beverages, promotion, equipment rentals, materials design and printing, ground transportation, insurance, legal counsel, permits, photocopying, signage, supplies, speaker fees, and videography, among other items. Timing and current circumstances will impact the overall budget, but the prior history will serve as a helpful guide to determine future spending. If your event is the first one, you'll have to rely on other events of similar size and scope to develop your budget. You should also consider developing a preliminary budget, obtaining bids from vendors with the understanding that you will make modifications as you near completion.

You'll also need to be in the mindset of controlling your expenses. Your preliminary budget will eventually become a "working" budget that should show "budgeted" line items versus "actual" expenses. This budget tracks revenue (e.g. sponsorships, registration fees, sales, etc.) and expenses, which will show net income and any losses. Monitoring the budget in real time will help you understand what's happening, and whether you are remaining under or headed over budget.

Should there be a budget shortfall or interest in pursuing more than your dollars will allow, you might consider sponsorships. We'll discuss this more in depth in the next chapter, but without sponsorships, many meetings and events are not financially viable.

## Human Capital

Many of my company's clients lack the sufficient internal staff to produce the event. Sometimes there is one or two people, maybe three at the most, who might handle the event's details. But often, these individuals have other job responsibilities—as evidenced by the case study. So it's critical to know if you will need additional staff to fully design and execute the event. The one aspect about managing events—one that many are unfamiliar with—is that they will end up consuming all your time. There are so many details that end up creating a life of their own that it's better to make sure you have the support needed to execute them.

If you don't have this support, I would consider working with an outside event management company that can offer the additional resources—and, often, perform them in less time given their expertise and capabilities. Companies like mine also employ volunteers to assist with select events, and provide the necessary training to ensure they execute where needed. Similar to budget, this is an area to seriously contemplate and be honest about. While some might think they don't have the budget to work with an outside company, or use volunteers to produce the event, you may end up finding that you can't afford *not* to—since human capital has the ability to compete with your organization's core capabilities.

## Expertise

"Anyone can do it." This is a phrase I often hear when it comes to managing events. For some reason, people think managing meetings and events is easy. That is, until they have to do it on their own—which undoubtedly changes their perspective. Designing and executing events is an art and a science. It takes precision and skilled expertise such as:

- Superior organizational skills
- Excellent communication
- Flexibility, creativity, and resourcefulness
- Strong project- and time-management skills
- Excellence in multitasking and delegation
- Exceptional people and diplomacy skills
- Grace and calm under pressure

When managing meetings and events, success is in executing the details. Many event professionals often manage multiple events simultaneously. It's event professionals who are in charge of educating their boss or client as to the details of events, and why they recommend the strategies they do. This requires diplomacy, sound judgement, listening, and strong people skills.

The profession can be compared to an orchestra. As the conductor leads the orchestra, he or she signals each of the other instruments into the music at designated times. The event professional does the same in working with colleagues, staff, vendors, bosses, clients, and other stakeholders in the process. It's up to event professionals to know whom they need to consult within the process and when.

Since no two events are alike, creativity is a critical skill for the event professional. Not only should you be able to explain the scope and purpose of an event, but you need ideas on how to design it to meet the organization's objectives. You should be able to take a vision and bring it to life. Tap into your creativity when troubleshooting or providing a quick solution to solve a problem. For instance, at one of our client events, we had a stage set that was built as part of a multi-day event. On the last day of the event, we entered the ballroom prior to the session to find that the staging had been removed overnight. It was unfortunately taken down too early and should have been done later that day. So our team scrambled to find some plants, chairs, pull-up banners, and other décor to fill in the space.

There are so many tasks to manage at any stage of the event designing process, which means you must know how to juggle. It's up to you to know how to effectively multitask and keep the event moving along simultaneously. Success lies in the ability to prioritize and focus without becoming distracted or overwhelmed. At all times, you must remain calm and in control—regardless of what's occurring. This means during the planning process and while the event is in progress.

While the right skills are essential, it's also important for the event professional to understand the nuances of the profession. For instance, we had a client whose annual conference was often over budget or just broke even each year. It also often blew its budget while the meeting was in progress, but didn't entirely understand why. After we began working with the client, we figured out that the former event manager hadn't accounted for the assessment of such fees as service charges, on top of hotel service costs. The client was always in a deficit from simply not knowing to include them in the original budget.

Alternatively, let's say you're planning for food and beverages, and you are scheduling host bars. There's a benchmark of planning for one bar per 75-100 guests, where you would use the lower figure if the guests tend to drink more. These are practices unique to the event management industry that many people do not know. Understanding how to perform them at any given time will be what brings your event success.

Knowing whom to work with is of equal importance. There are many different options for vendors who provide services to the events industry. This could be anything from ground transportation companies to translation services, photographers, caterers, printers, venues, and gift amenities, among many more. Most often, event professionals seek recommendations of reputable vendors.

This can work well and offer a firsthand account of how the vendor performs. It's also important for you to do your due diligence in assessing the right vendors as well. At my company, we established a preferred vendor program that has designated criteria and practices that determine suitability for the list. Since so many vendors have similar expertise, it's important for you to determine whether their practices will match the culture of your company as well as your meeting or event.

Working with vendor partners is the lifeblood of the event profession. Not having access to the right partners with stellar reputations can result in serious problems pulling off a successful program.

The event management profession has grown from relative obscurity to powerhouse status in delivering messages, transforming organizations, and changing lives. Passion is what fuels many event professionals who work unconventional hours and perform distinctive tasks. It's a profession that relies upon an abundance of resources and support to achieve success. That's why Resources is one of the most important parts of the SPARK Model$^{SM}$.

Another important resource is sponsorships, briefly mentioned earlier in this chapter. Without sponsorships, many meetings or events would not be financially possible. We'll take a closer look at those in the next chapter.

# Chapter 7

# Sponsorship Partners

**CASE STUDY**

*Sponsors are an important part of an event and can significantly strengthen the event's capabilities and reach. One of our clients hosts an annual conference where professionals gather to network, learn, share resources, and build their service centers to support their local communities. The conference relies on sponsorships to bring in revenue; however, the organization did not have as robust of a program nor the needed staff or mindset to grow the program to do more than break even. It often reached out to the same sponsors each year to cover the costs, but did not consider the possibility of the sponsor helping it grow as an organization. We worked with this organization to revamp its program to improve revenue growth, and target new sponsors and participants to attend the program. Our initial approach included:*

- *Analysis of a few prior years' sponsorship dollars to identify trends*
- *Research of relevant and related shows, and their sponsors, to create a target list of potential leads*
- *Target participants and exhibitors of other related shows*
- *Identification of other sectors that could be of potential benefit*

*We also provided input and adjustment to the sponsorship benefit levels and marketing materials to ensure engaging language that would capture the attention of the intended audiences and, more importantly, encourage them to act. In addition to establishing a stronger discovery foundation, we also employed a dedicated person who would conduct proactive and ongoing outreach to current sponsors and new ones. This person not only conducted internal research of potential targets, but also made calls to current and potential sponsors to identify their overall goals, objectives, and vision for the sponsorship. This helped us learn more about them, rather than simply telling them what we wanted them to know. We were then able to share how the sponsorship could help them reach their goals. As a result, we secured new participants, and the organization established a firm foundation for continued growth.*

There are some organizations that think sponsors for their event are the answer to making it a great success. While this might be true, it's important for you to conduct a needs assessment. Soliciting and securing sponsorships is hard. Gone are the days where companies simply gave you money because they thought you were a good cause. This certainly still happens, but today there is more competition than ever.

You should perform a needs assessment to ensure it's the right approach that will work for everyone. Consider thinking through the following when assessing the use of sponsors:

### What are your objectives for sponsorships?

You should spend time determining what you are interested in accomplishing through a sponsorship. It has to be more than just making money. The objectives should support your strategic plan and help push your organization forward. For instance, you might want to generate more awareness of your product, service, or issue. Every objective should be measurable and include specifics about timing and deliverables.

### Who is your target audience, and what do you want them to experience?

Sponsors are so much more than just an entity offering money for an event. In many instances, they're not even bringing *that* to the table, since their involvement may be in-kind. You should be thinking about whether there are sufficient prospects for sales as it relates to your target audience. That's why knowing your audience is so crucial, since you can build the sponsorship around the participant needs and interests—ultimately making it more memorable. For instance, I imagine you've attended conferences that feature great keynote speakers. Often, the sponsors are mentioned before the keynote, but that's not really what people want to hear. So you might consider the sponsor hosting a book signing (if the keynote has a book) or creating some form of educational content the participant can use that's related to the presentation. That's more memorable than just hearing the name of the sponsor, which often goes in one ear and out the other.

*Are sponsorship dollars or credibility needed?*

Many sponsors are not equipped to fund an event. There are some who bring credibility to the event given their well-respected stature or position within a certain industry. So they could potentially offer speakers and promote the event to their constituents—which could brand your event as a major player and help secure funding from other sources. Think through exactly what you need to best determine the level of partnership support.

*Do you have enough resources to execute a sponsorship program?*

The opening case study mentioned that the organization didn't have the internal and external resources to execute a sponsorship program. It takes time and dedicated resources to pull this off. For the best results, multiple people should be working the sponsorship end to cultivate the leads, keep in touch with sponsors, fulfill the benefit levels, and maintain overall communication. Many sponsor programs fail because of the lack of resources to consistently keep them in motion.

## Identifying Sponsors

There is so much competition for sponsors that it's become increasingly difficult to stand out from the crowd. That's why research is key to knowing whom you're targeting, finding other competing events, and learning sponsors' histories. For instance, if you're considering a community 5K, take a look at other 5K runs and their sponsors. Many different events or conferences are constantly being held. Simply do your homework in finding those related events and the type of companies that support them. This will not mean that those companies will definitely support your cause, but it at least gives you a place to start.

You should also consider local organizations in your community, such as the Chamber of Commerce or other business organizations related to your cause. Also, don't think that you need to have a big list. It takes precious time and resources to target companies that really don't have the ability to support your event. The list should be a qualified list of actual potential sponsors that you think will consider the sponsorship request. This includes companies that have been previous sponsors, or people or companies where there's a connection.

If you have additional resources, there are tools such as Hoovers Database that deliver comprehensive company, industry, and market intelligence to help identify prospects. This resource is definitely not required, but it can open up more opportunities. Make sure you research every company or person on your list. Having background information on the potential sponsor, its sponsorship practices, and past marketing efforts will go a long way in understanding its goals and if it is viable for your event. Look for reasons why it would benefit the potential sponsor to sponsor you. This will ultimately help with your sales pitch.

Do you like when people come up to you and ask for money? No small talk, just the question? I'm sure you don't—and neither do potential sponsorship prospects. Consider speaking with the sponsor about its goals and whom it is trying to reach. If it will share an overall budget with you, that will be key. Approach it from the standpoint of "consulting" rather than selling. The point is, you want to draw a correlation as to how your sponsorship will help it reach its goals. Knowing the sponsor's vision will help you construct a proposal that speaks to its needs and positions you to become a partner in its success. It definitely takes more time to focus this way, but it works.

## Building the Sponsorship Program

Once you identify the sponsor's overall vision, goals, and interests, develop a proposal that outlines the discussion, what you intend to offer, and what it will receive. You should include sponsorship terms and overall instructions of how it will be executed. Your proposal should also detail any additional costs or services the sponsor is required to contribute so everyone is on the same page. Most sponsorships will require time and commitment to ensure you arrive at what will work for both parties. Keep in mind, not all sponsorships are monetary-based. It's up to your team to decide which sponsors will be needed to enhance your credibility and consult with them accordingly. Identifying what they will bring to the table is the same type of discussion as that of outlining funds to be provided. In fact, it might be even more critical to define exactly how the sponsor will interact with the overall program.

For instance, when producing the Cocoa Symposium, we had many partner sponsors whose expertise and names were used for the event. In this instance, they offered featured presenters to share their topical expertise about the cocoa crop, and we could promote the event to their organizations' stakeholders as well. Because of their reputation and leadership within the industry, the symposium benefited from having their involvement—which raised the profile of the event and generated increased exposure of the outcomes.

Once you have an idea on how to build a mutually beneficial sponsorship program that can benefit both you and your prospect, decide on the benefit levels. Keep in mind, when consulting with the prospective sponsor, you'll need to remain open in devising the benefit levels—since they should be customized to the sponsor's needs. However, you can have some basic thoughts in mind. For instance, you might establish levels such as Platinum—$25,000; Gold—$15,000; Silver—$10,000; or Presenting Sponsor—$50,000. By no means are these level amounts set in stone. This is just an example of the value of some types of sponsorships.

Depending on your event, the amounts might be much lower, or potentially higher. The intent is for the higher sponsor levels to receive more benefits with the sponsorship, and the lower amounts to receive fewer. As an example, Platinum level sponsors might have their logo on all materials, a speaking opportunity at the event, their company name and logo in all promotions, a display booth at the event, their product featured prominently in high traffic areas, etc. The lower amounts would receive fewer benefits. But again, it's important to spend time thinking through what you envision proper benefit levels to be while remaining open to customization for maximum sponsor impact.

## Sponsor Communications

As you sign on sponsors and begin working with them, be careful not to let your sponsors seize control of your program. Undoubtedly, you want them involved and to have a great partnership where everyone benefits. But there are some instances where the sponsor might attempt to exert control over all decisions and influence every facet of the event. That's why it's so important to outline the details of each organization's role, so the rules of engagement are totally clear. You want sponsors to feel ownership of their role in the program, but not take full ownership in deciding how the program will run, who will be involved, what other sponsors will be doing, etc.

That being said, communication is critical. Once the sponsor is on board, establish a set schedule for discussing the sponsorship and keeping the sponsor informed of overall plans. I've seen some companies get a commitment from a sponsor, and then that's it. They don't reach out to the sponsor or keep it updated about details until closer to the event date. And, even worse, they don't follow up after the event, either.

So, just as you are planning every detail of your event, the sponsor part will need to have its own level of planning effort. This could be in the form of a regularly scheduled call or recap emails of progress made to date. Basically, manage expectations. Sponsors should receive a timeline, especially since you'll need to obtain either funds, products, or people (e.g. speakers) from them—and they'll need time on their end to plan the fulfillment. They also should be a part of your promotion efforts. Some sponsors record short videos of their prior and current involvement, or they may offer some form of teaser or promotional gift that participants should know about. Those types of details need to be worked out in advance so they match your promotional efforts and give sponsors enough time to plan them into their work flow.

Another major factor to consider is making sure your sponsors know about other potential sponsors you plan to solicit. This really should be discussed at the beginning of the consultation phase, as it will need to be defined before they come on board. For instance, for certain events I've planned, we've had sponsors mention they couldn't be a sponsor if one of their competitors would be involved. For many events, you'll need to think through the categories of sponsorships and the cost of having just one major sponsor for particular areas. Sometimes, this just isn't possible and it will limit your event. That's why it's important to identify this early on and keep moving to find those sponsors that are fine with having competitors at the event to help grow your sponsorship base.

Also keep in mind that some sponsors may not share the same philosophy, which could also prohibit their involvement. For instance, we often see nowadays how political discourse has impacted many events. We had an event scheduled for Indianapolis a few years ago during Indiana's anti-gay religious freedom law. Many people canceled events, travel to Indiana was banned, and sponsors pulled out from select events. The issue was resolved by the time our event took place, but there were discussions and consideration whether the event would still go on. The same can be said for sponsors who may disagree with other sponsoring companies. For instance, maybe one company uses animals for experiments, and another disagrees with this. That's why it's important to be transparent at the outset to help avoid any potential controversy.

## Retaining Your Sponsors

If your event is a multi-year program, you should have a strategy for securing and maintaining sponsors. As you develop a program, you should think through how you will evaluate success. Start with your defined goals and objectives. Take the time to talk with your sponsors after the event, either in-person or via conference call. I know many organizations that don't talk to their sponsors at all after the event, only to reach out to them for the next event later the following year. Doing this doesn't show much appreciation for your sponsors' role in your event.

Perhaps you speak with not only your sponsors, but your own staff, select individuals from the sponsors' target markets, and others to obtain a wide range of opinions on sponsorship effectiveness. In addition to personally speaking with sponsors, you might consider using an electronic survey for the other individuals and groups. Include questions about the sponsorships in your event's general survey. Additionally, ask your sponsors for internal tracking information about their sponsorship to see how they measure success.

While in the evaluation phase, timing is everything. Make sure to send a follow-up to sponsors. Within about 48 hours, forward a snapshot of the event that includes success points, number of attendees, dollars raised (if applicable), or other specific results-oriented points and a few photos specific to that sponsor. This helps to show the sponsors you care about and appreciate their involvement in the event. You should then consider a thank you gift that's personalized with a handwritten note, or a phone call and certain type of memorabilia from the event that may be specific to the sponsor. It shows that you care and have taken the time to recognize sponsors for their important involvement in your program.

If there are follow-up communications after the event, your sponsors should be included in them so they can continue to reap the benefits of their investment. It's also important to continue the conversation with them. Don't just forget about them since the event is over. Use the time to cultivate the relationship by incorporating them throughout your continued communications. By keeping them in the loop about what your organization is doing, this may give them additional ideas and desires to remain active with your company or organization—and potentially be involved with other programs throughout the year.

It's about relationship, not just a transaction. As I've mentioned before, I see this often with organizations where there is no continued connection or attention to the sponsors. Just think about how much further your organization could be if you dedicated more time to nurturing the sponsor partners rather than using them for a cyclical period of time.

Invite them to lunch, if they are located in your area, or schedule a time to speak with them once a month or every six weeks. Send them a note of something that may interest them, and if you come across something that's related to your event they sponsored, by all means reach out to them with the information. Think of sponsorship outreach as a communications program, rather than just another piece of the event puzzle.

When you build your sponsorship to provide participants with an optimum experience, there will always be opportunities for continued discussion. Keep up with your participants, allowing them a time to respond to their overall experience with the event. Sift through the stories received to populate your communications with them, or potentially even produce a video that can be used for future communications to promote the event. The key is to keep pushing your communications messages to promote the event and retain your sponsors well into the future.

# Chapter 8

# Pre-Event Coordination

**CASE STUDY**

*An international organization based in Paris, France, contacted my company to produce a high- level forum to analyze how large-scale restoration of ecosystems can stimulate sustainable development. The international conference took place at the National Academy of Sciences in Washington, D.C., and convened scientists, practitioners, NGOs, business leaders, and policymakers. My team began working with the client by establishing a timeline of all pertinent details to serve as the conference work plan to cater to a short lead time conference. These details included every piece of information, from website launch to when packages could be sent to the venue, to where shuttle buses could drop guests off to when Twitter posts would be released to when rooms would be set for the conference. The timeline was a working document that was updated daily to ensure all details were captured and gaps filled. It was also a document we shared with all members of the planning team, including the client, so everyone was on the same page. This event also had a short lead time, which required that we hold regular planning meetings with the client—but at unique times to accommodate the time difference in Paris.*

*Once we confirmed the venue, our team began the details of populating a staging guide, which included all details related to the event venue such as placement of chairs, tables, audio-visual equipment, security details, etc. This was different from the timeline in that it was information specifically for the venue to help it set the spaces to our needs and requirements. We also began hosting meetings with other partners, including the audio-visual and production teams, and managed select speaker details. The speakers required that we work with their assistants, since many traveled often and were not available to field requests for information. Our team also managed the printing of special signage in our area to avoid any potential issues with customs in having to ship from Paris last minute. We also prepared handout materials and established a social media marketing outreach effort to build excitement and engagement for the conference, and to increase participation.*

*Our social media team worked with the client on discussing the intended messages and outcomes from the outreach. From this discussion, the messages were refined and a targeted list developed to begin communicating the conference details. We developed an HTML invitation as well as a series of posts to begin promotions. We also reached out to speakers and their institutions directly via their Twitter handles to build awareness and interest in attending among their Twitter followers while employing the use of photos and video to help bolster the message.*

*From registration to logistical coordination, production of materials, stage set design, and marketing and promotions, all details were simultaneously in motion. Our team served as the engine in leading, guiding, and directing all conference steps. As a result, this last-minute conference featured 700 international guests and 52 speakers from 15 different countries who collected and promoted innovative ideas and tools on how to implement effective large-scale ecosystem restoration projects.*

The "A" in the SPARK Model℠ stands for Activations. This means you begin execution of the details related to the purpose and objectives defined at the beginning of your planning process. As the case study demonstrated, there were multiple pieces of the puzzle occurring simultaneously.

And as the event manager, it's your job to think through each of the details and set the plan in motion. The most worthwhile amount of time that you should spend managing an event is developing the timeline. This document helps you think through the event from the participant perspective, and will alert you to any gaps in coverage or details while establishing the timing and pace or tempo. The case study conference was an event planned in approximately 6-7 weeks, so the timing was short for that level of activity. This is why one of the first questions you ask when planning an event should be, "When will the event take place?"

Once the timeframe is established, that will dictate how and when other planning aspects will occur. This also includes your personal planning time. With pre-event meetings, site visits, meetings with vendors, and ongoing communications, this adds up. This is often why clients tend to contract with my company, since many don't anticipate how much an event can overrun their schedule. The workload requires more than a full-time job. While costs and budgeting are often considerations, it's important to think through how much time you have to manage the event, and how much time it will take from your regular schedule.

In addition to those times, you'll also need to think through the space you intend to use that will be impacted by the time. For instance, if your event is last minute, you may not have as many options for a venue. Or, what happens when the building contact suddenly needs to limit the time vendors can enter a building for setup? At my company, we have experienced many situations as such hosting events in the Washington, D.C., area—especially using unique spaces such as the Capitol building. During one of the many events we hosted at the Capitol, our truck with equipment needed to undergo a security sweep by the Secret Service at a location that was not in the same location as the Capitol. While our truck arrived in the early morning hours well in advance, it still became held up at the security facility, and did not move for at least two hours. When they finally released the truck, the equipment made it to the room of the breakfast, where setup began under an extremely condensed timeframe. As guests began to walk into the room, the crew had just finalized installation of the large screen and other equipment—only to quickly scramble to hide other equipment and exit the room.

When choosing a venue, the details related to it will affect the time invested in using the space, creating a correlation between time and space. With the heightened security on Capitol Hill, there are additional restrictions and limitations that come with the space, affecting the overall invested planning time and potential tempo or pace of the event. We'll discuss tempo more in the next chapter, but that's another significant consideration of the pre-event planning—especially in managing the "run of show" or event flow from moment to moment.

When developing the timeline, start backward from your event date. This will build a more realistic picture of what you're able to get done and when. Then, think through every possible detail related to coordinating the event, and include it on your timeline. For instance, if you're looking for a venue, your timeline might include:

- Week of May 15
  Develop list of 3-5 potential venues

- Week of May 15
  Draft request for proposal (RFP)

- Week of May 22
  Distribute RFP

- Week of May 29
  Deadline to receive RFPs

- Week of June 7
  Review responses, conduct due diligence

- Week of June 15
  Make selection on venue

As you get more of the tasks in place, you may be able to see running themes that allow you to group several tasks under a category header, such as Site Selection, Venue Logistics, Materials Development, or Marketing Outreach, among others. Take your time to think through every possible action. You'll be thankful you did when other items come up that can just plug into what you've already created.

**The Team**

Since managing events involves so many different partners, it's important that everyone is on the same page at all times. The best way to achieve this is by holding regular planning meetings. These could be weekly, bi-weekly, monthly, or at other intervals—depending on the event date and staff resources. These planning meetings should detail where you are in the life cycle of the planning process. I recommend having a regular internal meeting, and a meeting with your client if you're planning the event on behalf of an organization or company. Otherwise, an internal meeting would suffice—but make sure to include any vendor partners at designated times so they too can hear the details and offer any input on their role as needed.

As the event manager, keep in mind that you should populate your team with professionals within the industry. This applies whether you work with full-time or part-time professionals, volunteers, vendor partners, or others involved with the program. This means that you should be careful about micromanaging the event. As an event manager, it can be in our DNA to try to control every single facet of the event. But that's simply not possible. Attempting to control everything and everyone will not only make you bogged down and ineffective as a manager, but it will frustrate your team as well. It's important for you to be confident about whom you work with so they can perform to their professional ability. Your role is to be a team leader who can coach people, things, and situations. But trying to do everything on your own will not only endanger yourself and demoralize your team, but potentially result in an unsuccessful program. Make sure the right people are around you, and trust them.

## Logistics

As you work through your timeline, executing each detail will begin the longest planning period. Depending on your event, one of your first steps will be to identify a destination and locate a venue. Once you begin working with the venue's details, this will take you through the entire period of planning the event. Additional aspects related to the venue will include accommodating what will happen at the venue. For instance, you'll need to address such questions as:

- What will be the overall flow of the event?
- What type of room arrangements will be needed?
- Will sleeping rooms be needed?
- What type of audio-visual equipment will be required?
- Will there be any entertainment? If so, what type and what equipment will be needed?
- Is there any special insurance needed for outside entertainment?
- What type of food and beverage functions will be required?

These are just some of the questions that will ultimately lead to others, and they will largely depend on the type of meeting or event being planned. But you're entering the weeds where every major or minor detail will need to be identified, probed, and managed. Use your timeline daily to identify what you need to focus on and when. At one time, it might be working with the venue on logistical details; at another time, it might be working specifically with the audio-visual crew or running reports on registrations and RSVPs. Your timeline is your lifeline. Keep it close and refer to it early and often. It should also be updated to accommodate real-time information and changes, and make sure to share it with the rest of the team.

Depending on the type of event you're planning, you'll work with other vendors during this phase, such as ground transportation companies, catering, equipment rental, travel, gift and amenity providers, entertainment, sign language interpreters, audio-visual equipment, and the list goes on. Each of these aspects should fit on your timeline and have specific planning details related to them, specifically what you need to do to secure them for the event.

## Marketing

Just as much planning that goes into the logistical side should be applied to marketing. Knowing your audience and firmly understanding your objectives will help serve as a guide in executing targeted strategies. For instance, many organizations think they need to use Facebook, Twitter, or other types of social media to promote their events. This might be true for some organizations, but if your target audience doesn't use Twitter, then why consider it? Here's a marketing checklist to get you started on developing a robust marketing outreach:

- Define your goals and objectives for marketing (e.g. increase awareness, generate sales, etc.)
- Identify your target market
- Adopt a theme (if applicable)
- Develop a budget
- Establish multiple touch points to reach audiences (e.g. email, social media, public relations, video, etc.)
- Identify organizational spokesperson(s)
- Conduct follow-up
- Evaluate

Each phase of this marketing outreach will prepare you for better results. And the sooner it's started, the better. There are some events that require promotions to start a year in advance, with periodic activity occurring throughout the year. However, there may be others that will suffice in 40-60 days. The point is to know your audience and type of event to best leverage getting attention.

## Goals and Objectives

Think through what you want to accomplish through your marketing. The case study revealed that the client wanted to build awareness of the conference to produce interest and increase participation. It chose to do this through launching a social media campaign. By the time the conference ended, it had almost 700 participants. Because of the engagement, the conference reached its overall objectives and delivered innovative ideas on how to build more sustainable ecosystems. You'll remember at the opening of the book, a gentleman learned an idea at a conference to reduce homelessness in his state of Utah. It was a monumental undertaking that produced life-changing results. The same can be said for this conference discussing ecosystems, which is why it's so important to make sure you provide the right platform and market your program to achieve potentially transformative results.

## Identify Your Target Market

There are some industries that are small, and others that might be quite expansive. But not everyone is your target. It's important that you identify who is the right audience for your message. In thinking about your goals and who can help you reach them, start with a database of prospects. Perhaps these are clients, members of your organization or prospects, volunteers, and customers. Look for the type of individual who, if multiplied, would help you reach your goal. For instance, people who are currently using a certain product, or have expertise in the discipline of your organization, or who might have expressed interest at some point in wanting more information from your company or organization. Group them in categories by further dissecting their practices. If you know they're repeat customers, how much have they bought, and what types of items are they interested in? Or, if they volunteered with your organization, how often did they volunteer, and what was their principal role? This type of targeting will determine the type of profile you need to achieve your goal.

## Adopt a Theme (if applicable)

A theme can be used for any type of event that even might tie in with a national effort, such as American Heart Month. A theme is a way to brand your organization and strengthen the connection with your audience. For instance, my team assisted with rebranding a client's national conference that had grown somewhat stale and predictable. It operated in the same capacity each year with no new members, sponsors, or alternative ways of delivering its information. One of our suggestions was to rename the conference something other than "annual conference" and tie in a theme that members could adopt and embrace. This has given the organization a fresh delivery that creates more ownership from the members as well as encourages a call to action.

## Develop a Budget

It's important to know what resources you have to support marketing outreach. While there's a considerable amount that can be done for free, such as email marketing, you might need to use other ways to target your intended audiences. Whether developing materials for mail, purchasing paid Facebook ads, incorporating advertising, or other means, you'll need a budget. This is what makes knowing your audience members so critical in how they receive information.

Don't spend resources in areas that won't bring you a return. There's no need to incorporate the latest and greatest "shiny objects" that everyone thinks you should. Develop your budget around your targets so you can best reach them.

**Identify the Organizational Spokesperson(s)**

There are some organizations that have an established person who speaks on their behalf. This might be someone within the organization or perhaps even yourself, a celebrity, sponsors, or another designated representative. These individuals will be key to generating awareness of the event, and will need talking points and direction about when and how they will be used. Much like the general work plan, a timeline and activities plan should be produced.

**Follow Up and Evaluate**

As you develop your marketing program, consistent and proactive follow-up is important to ensure your messages are working and target audiences are engaged. Over the years, I have found that many organizations don't follow up with participants of their events after it's all said and done. And what a missed opportunity that is, as it could mean the difference between leaving money on the table and not having your service or issue at the forefront of those who may need it most. Whether through email, mail, or the tools that resonate with your target audience, reach out to them about the event and continue the conversation. Depending on the type of event you produce, it would be worthwhile to extend an offer or solicit some form of call to action.

These strategies will also help with evaluating how well the marketing efforts worked. Did you increase the number of participants at your event, if that was the objective? What about increasing revenue or generating more awareness for your issue or product? What email and messaging worked best? The success of your effort will stem from your objectives. Identifying what works and what doesn't will put you in a stronger position to build on your success for the next time.

Spending quality time in your research and objective phase will better prepare you for the planning phase. Use of timing and space will affect every decision related to your event. You'll then be faced with the actual flow, which sets all plans in motion.

# Chapter 9

# The Event Flow and Post-Event

**CASE STUDY**

*It was a night to celebrate 30 years of a corporation's notable achievements, and it was a great honor for my company to be the event producer. After several months of planning, it was finally showtime, and every fine detail and intimate element was planned and ready to be executed. The president of the organization had extremely demanding tastes, so we knew it was important that everything went without a hitch. The evening would feature reminiscing about times past and how far the company had come. Every moment of the evening was choreographed on the event script, starting with shuttle bus departures from the company headquarters to the venue—which was a national music performing arts center. As guests began to arrive, they were greeted by a welcome table, where their names were checked against a list and name badges distributed. They were also offered a coat check and parking voucher if they used the parking facility instead of the shuttles.*

Guests were then directed down a hallway flagged by posters of old and new images of the corporation. On the way to the reception, they enjoyed music by the Andes Manta band playing music indigenous to Peru. A very large projection screen hung from the ceiling and displayed, photos of the people and faces from the organization past and present. There were two full bars open with passed hors d'oeuvres for guests to enjoy. Once the hour-long reception concluded, chimes rang to indicate guests should move downstairs for the dinner. There was a dramatic entry into the dinner space as guests descended a series of steps to see an ornately decorated stage featuring a gobo-projected I Ching symbol that had special meaning to the founders of the organization. There were also other stage elements, including a screen for video adorned by a bonsai tree.

There was no podium, only the stage that featured the CEO, who shared opening remarks and invited guests to dinner. Upon conclusion of the dinner, the program began, featuring a commemoration video and remarks from one of the founders of the corporation. The program was unconventional in that it didn't feature prepared remarks; rather, guests were invited to the stage or at their tables to share personal reflections about their time at the company. The CEO then closed the program, and guests began to depart. Some were invited to another lounge within the music center for an after-party reception, and departing guests were given a departing gift—a book by a Pulitzer Prize-winning author who was also on the company's board. The guests were in awe of the evening, and while our team heard many comments throughout the event, one guest's remarks *stood out when referencing the company's CEO: "Wow, she really knows how to throw a party."*

*After the event, a debrief was held with the client to determine what went well and to conduct any follow-up of reconciling invoices, sending out thank you notes/additional gifts, touching base with vendors, ensuring any items delivered to the event were returned, and other activities as designated.*

The event experience for your guests is represented in every detail, from the moment they receive the invitation to arriving onsite when the event is in motion. After months of preparation, the actual flow of the event will be a "show" of its own. The "K" in the SPARK Model$^{SM}$ stands for Know-How. It's the expertise and skills to not only design and plan, but to execute and evaluate in positioning your organization to continue building effective programs. In the last chapter, we discussed elements of timing and space and the reliance on each. We also touched upon the pace at which the event elements are placed into action. While the case study described the actual moments during the event, there are other aspects of tempo to consider, such as during the design phase and whether it's the right time to focus on select tasks. For instance, if you haven't yet secured the venue for an event, but you want to release the details, sending a "save-the-date" would suffice in getting on participant calendars until all details are finalized.

Understanding your target audience will help you design the tempo. For instance, if you are serving a dinner and a headliner VIP will be the keynote presenter, but the person will need to leave immediately after speaking to catch a flight, then you'll need to factor that into your details on how to make sure you start on time and keep things moving. Or what about the student who will deliver a scientific presentation in a scholarship competition, who practices certain religious observances? These observances dictate that the student can't work after the sun goes down, and the presentation was scheduled for 7:00 p.m. This happened during one of my company's events, so we had to speed up the tempo of the program to best accommodate this student.

There are also other times where a presenter or entertainer doesn't show or is running late. In those instances, you'll need to adjust the program to either move on to another section or slow things down to meet the need.

So, how exactly do you prepare for the event flow?

In the last chapter, I mentioned that one of the tasks where you should spend a good amount of time is on developing the work plan/timeline. That exercise is to identify all tasks related to the event that will directly impact the flow on the event day. Another planning tool to develop is what's called a "Run of Show." The run of show is a document that outlines the entire script for the event, from start to finish. You can think of it as a further fleshed out version of your timeline. Using the timeline as the foundation, you can fill in more detail underneath each of the tasks to provide further instruction on what will take place that day.

To get a better understanding of a run of show, take a look at the following example:

5:45pm    Shuttle #1 departs company headquarters for venue

6:15pm    Shuttle #2 departs hotel for venue

6:30pm    Shuttle #1 makes its second departure from company headquarters for venue

6:45pm    Shuttle #2 makes its second departure from hotel for venue

6:15pm   Guests begin to arrive and proceed to a welcome table, where they are warmly greeted by company staff. After having their name checked on the RSVP list, guests are given a name badge and instructed to inspect the badge for indication of their table assignment. They are offered coat check, asked if they need parking validation, then directed down the hall to the reception, passing the images on easels representing the company's milestone years.

The process would continue from there until the very end of the evening. One important aspect is to lead with high energy at your event. Given the many different types of events, this will mean something different for each event manager. But you want people to be excited to attend, and interested in remaining throughout the day. We discussed earlier in Chapter 5 how to build your event to speak to the five senses. In the event flow, this is where it comes to life in leading with power and ending with a call to action. Regardless of the type of event you are hosting— whether for your church, a local community organization, or a Fortune 500 company—it's so important to know your audience and grab their attention immediately, keeping them engaged throughout the event's progression. For instance, there are some events that feature comedians or motivational speakers at the beginning of select events. Others may have an entertainer or someone who can ramp up the energy right out of the gate. This helps to immediately draw people into your event to attract, engage, and inspire.

But don't be concerned if those types of elements are not right for your event. This certainly doesn't mean that your event won't be interesting or engaging. It will just be important for you to determine what that right feature is to be successful. Perhaps it's a leading expert in a certain field, or perhaps it's a "field trip" to a destination related to your field or an interactive activity. It will really depend on what you're trying to accomplish, balanced with your resources, ingenuity, and capabilities.

While it's important to lead with high energy or an informative, engaging structure, it's equally important for the day (or days) to flow with what's important to your organization. Not too long ago, my company began working with an organization that had a conference agenda with no breaks built in. This changed after we started working with the organization, but such a small (and large) detail can have a dramatic effect on whether your event will be successful. If people continue to leave during the sessions to use the restrooms or check their emails, return calls, etc., then that's a major indication that a change is needed in the overall program. It also compromises your event flow, given there is no time to absorb the information—no matter how great it might have been—nor an opportunity to network. This can be the equivalent of simply yelling at someone without listening.

If networking is an important part of your event, it needs to be built into the program. Otherwise, your event will have the potential to not achieve its goals. This, too, is why it's important to know your overall objectives so you can measure whether they've been achieved.

Equally important for your event flow is to leave your participants with a call to action. This simply means you should want people to be motivated to continue the conversation after the event. Perhaps you introduced a new product, celebrated a company anniversary, held a multi- day conference to explore topical areas of cocoa, or had another focus. The key is building how you want people to continue to engage with your organization or brand after the event. This is often a missed opportunity with many events. Once it's all said and done, everyone goes about their merry way, and organizations don't ask for their continued engagement.

This should be a part of building the objectives for your event. At the beginning, you should be thinking through what it is that you want people to do. For instance, do you have an online community that discusses your topical area? Perhaps you engage people to become a part of it and promote it throughout your event. There are so many ways to continue the engagement; it'll be important to think through what that means to your organization.

From a logistical standpoint in building your event flow, many event managers often keep many of the details in their head. However, this can sometimes cause the manager to overlook elements that are critical in the process and that may present a gap. One of the best ways to counter this approach is to assign a deputy to assist with the details and flesh out a run of show for the program. This way, should anything happen, someone else can step in to keep items moving forward.

This process also highlights the importance of having regular meetings during the planning phase, which has been previously discussed. Whether it's monthly, bi-weekly, weekly, or daily, as you get closer to the event, having all hands on deck dissecting each detail is important. While some may think it's overkill to have frequent meetings, they are an absolute necessity. At any given time, something could go off the rails while planning, and it's better to know sooner than later.

If you have speakers, VIPs, or other presenters at your events, it's important to think through how they will be managed during the day. For instance, in my company, we have managed events featuring federal government officials, as well as those from around the world. While managing those types of individuals will likely involve the Secret Service and other security professionals, you might run into the same with renowned performers or corporate CEOs of major companies, among others. The point is to think through how you will accommodate them. Will there be a special holding room? How will they enter the premises— for instance, via private car service? Which entrance will the car service deliver them to onsite? Once out of the car, which way will they walk to the holding room? Will there be a restroom in the holding room or nearby for them to refresh themselves? What about food and other amenities, and those who will be allowed to greet the VIP? You'll need to flesh out those particular details to execute onsite.

On a similar note, another aspect to consider is whether you will need to schedule a rehearsal before the event begins. In my company, we have scheduled many rehearsals of our events prior to the event or on the morning of the event, depending on when the event began. This is a wonderful exercise, as you get to see the program in motion and can adjust and adapt as needed. This sometimes means that you'll have to rent the space in advance of the event as well, so you can conduct the practice in the same space. But this could impact your cost, so keep that in mind. Ideally, however, it's better to host the rehearsal as far in advance as possible so you have time to make any adjustments.

Also, remember to have a plan B, and even C, in place. Things often occur while the event's in motion, so you want to be prepared and have several backups just in case. For instance, what happens if your prized speaker or performer is a no-show? What will you do if the power goes out, or your ground transportation vendor goes into receivership just a few minutes before having to pick up guests? We'll discuss this a little more in the next chapter, but those are the types of situations that you want to be prepared for during execution.

If you are not managing events on a regular basis, I can understand if the run of show document is a little bit intimidating. But just think of it as an extension of your timeline. I want to highlight this again because it really becomes almost a therapeutic exercise in thinking about your event in minute-by-minute terms. This will undoubtedly help you become a better manager of your time, resources, vendors, and delivery of the engagement. Think about the last event you might have attended. What do you think went well? What do you think went not so well? Were you engaged? Did it keep you excited, and was it a very informative program? The answers to these questions will rely heavily on the upfront planning of your run of show and timeline.

So take your time in building your timeline, which will lead to your run of show. Every event is different and will have varying objectives, features, elements, and practices. But you definitely want to start out with high energy to capture the participants and then build your program to speak to those important aspects your audience needs to hear. It'll then be important to follow up with a call to action to continue the conversation.

**Post Event**

After it's over, there are always large sighs of relief, excitement, and pride for what you've accomplished. And rightfully so, given the complexity of many events and their overall impact. But this phase also comes with some hefty "to-do's" as well, so it's not quite the time to celebrate just yet.

You'll remember at the beginning of this book, the overall discussion about setting your objectives and making sure they are measurable? Well, the purpose of measurable objectives is so you can evaluate whether they were met during the post-event phase. For instance, there are some organizations or companies that might conduct a pre-event survey to determine how much participants may know about the subject. Those same companies may also conduct a post-event survey at the end to see how any perspectives might have changed, stayed the same—or they may measure another conclusion. Many organizations conduct general evaluations of the event at the end. But this is still an area that should be determined at the beginning of the planning phase so you know what you're trying to measure,

These types of surveys are often generated electronically. In some instances, and depending on the stakeholder, some organizations reach out personally to key stakeholder groups to get their immediate and personalized feedback. This could be especially helpful with sponsors, as mentioned in the Sponsorships chapter. Another way to gather feedback is to conduct a formal debrief meeting with those involved in the event's production. For instance, at JDC Events, we often conduct debrief meetings with our clients at the end of each event. We also do the same with any vendors associated with the event. We work with many different vendors at different times, so it's important for us to know what worked, what didn't, and how we can improve upon any practices in the future. From these debriefs, we develop after action reports that detail the event's scope, results, and next steps to improve upon the event if it will happen again.

Understand that there will be considerable follow-up to do after the event; however, it's critical that you start jotting debrief notes immediately after the event. This is when the event is the freshest in your mind, and you'll be in the best place to recall activities. These can also be used as talking points for when you hold a more formal debrief with the planning team. The same can be said for those in the planning process. Ask them the same questions, such as what went well, what you would do different next time, and other specific questions related to your event's details. Give these individuals a certain amount of time to respond to your request so you can build an electronic file. Then, once you all meet together, the notes from the initial feedback can populate the agenda during your discussion.

I have worked with many organizations that did not conduct a debrief at all, or they did it well after the event had occurred. There are disadvantages in doing this, given that memories are short and those involved may not remember key points that could be critical to improving upon a reoccurring event. But if you collect the data, it's important to use it so your company or organization can move forward and ensure it's meeting its goals.

Also keep in mind during the debrief phase that this is not the time to beat yourself up on anything that might have gone wrong. That's why it'll be important to start the debrief process with your successes to set the tone.

In addition to debrief activities, there will be other tasks to close out the event process. These might include sending thank you notes to your clients, vendors, or any other special guests. We are currently living in a digital age where everything is done electronically. However, I encourage you to handwrite personalized thank you notes that even capture something specific about the person you're sending it to. It's such a lost art to send a note in the mail, but I guarantee you that it does get noticed, especially since everyone else is sending their mail electronically. This type of gesture will help ensure a positive message for your event, and might even lead to repeat sponsorship or other business related to your event.

# Chapter 10

# Expect the Unexpected

**CASE STUDY**

*A client hosted a five-day international symposium on veterinary medicine at a hotel in Washington, D.C. This event hosted approximately 300 people, and there were many moving parts to the symposium such as poster presentations, receptions, live animals, and an off-site session held at a university location of one of the partnering organizations.*

*The day that participants would travel to the off-site presentation began with several sessions at the hotel. The lunch would be hosted at the university location, and then participants would have a chance to hear from the presenter. The registration materials identified that the special session would be taking place and that lunch would be served. Participants also had the opportunity to sign up to attend the session. However, the program books were printed by the host organization and did not clearly feature the presentation session as being held at an off-site location. This site required participants to board a shuttle bus for a short trip to the university location, and then they would be transported back upon return. We included an insert to help convey this detail.*

*However, we noticed when the buses were staged that not many people were showing up to board. Our team was already at the location, and once the organizer and about 10-15 other individuals arrived, it seemed there were no other participants scheduled to attend. The room was set for 150 people, and included the same for lunch. As it turned out, most of the participants thought it was a half-day event and ended up having lunch on their own and going to tour Washington, D.C.*

*Meanwhile, the session presenter delivered his talk to approximately twenty or so people. Needless to say, the presenter was furious at the miscommunication, as this was his opportunity to deliver his subject matter expertise to such a distinguished audience. It was indeed an extremely uncomfortable and sorrowful outcome. Although the materials would be given to participants the next day, the damage had clearly been done.*

Whether the audience knows it or not, there is always something unexpected that happens at an event. It's just the nature of the profession. While some incidents may be more painful than others, it still doesn't minimize their impact. Even the best event manager will not be able to control everything. But you can at least try to buffer their impact by embracing the possibilities and thinking ahead.

It's funny—early in my event profession, I thought about things that could occur and wondered why in the world I wanted to do this. I guess the event's overall impact is what mostly drove my inspiration. But, you really need to have the stomach to think about the "what-ifs." Especially after the terrorist attacks of September 11, 2001, we are now living in a time that seems to be more dangerous and susceptible to outside influences hampering our profession. Gone are the days of just worrying about a fire, miscommunication that leads to an empty room, the power going out, or other technology failures. There are now more opportunities for severe weather, active shooters, and civil unrest, among other crises to have an impact on your event.

It's clear that we will not be able to control every unfortunate incident that might occur. But there are a few things that can be done to at least consider the possibilities. Event managers and producers must look beyond the typical logistical coordination as the main authority for an event. There are varying degrees of the "unexpected" and "emergencies." While they are the same in terms of their impact, there are different ways to respond to every situation. Let's first look at emergencies that have the potential to be life-threatening. Developing a thorough emergency procedures document is essential in identifying and planning for the possibilities.

## EMERGENCY PROCEDURES

### Pre-Planning Phase

- Conduct an assessment of the potential risk. For instance, if your event is being held in a hurricane-prone location, and it is hurricane season, you would want to think through options should one occur. You should invest in taking the time to conduct this assessment. It's not something where you just think about it one afternoon. You should engage your team to come up with scenarios that are pertinent to your particular event. I am reminded of the time we conducted an assessment with a client. We took the time to think through every possible scenario, and then countered it with a response. This also included the venue contact and other partners in our event as well. It took time, but it at least gave us a solid starting point to understand how we might deal with any unfortunate incidents.

- Whenever there might be an issue with a vendor contract, one of my attorneys would first always say, "What does the contract say?" This is always a good reminder to ensure that your contracts have cancellation clause protections. For hotels, they are often called "Force Majeure" clauses, and they have stipulations of what you can do should incidents occur that require you to cancel your event. However, other vendors will have alternate types of clauses that you should make sure are included to provide additional protections.

- I was in New York for a client's event, and it was during the timeframe of the 10-year anniversary of the September 11th terrorist attacks. We were doing a site visit of the hotel, and just as I was about to ask the hotel contact about emergency procedures, an alarm of some sort sounded. It wasn't a loud fire alarm, but it was enough to make you wonder what it was. So I continued to ask about emergency procedures especially in light of the alarm going off, and the representative looked at me and said, "Honey, I have no idea...you'll have to ask security about that." I was so stunned to hear such a response, especially during the time of the 10-year anniversary of the September 11th attacks.

It's important to ask venues about their emergency procedures, and hopefully you'll receive a better response than I did from that hotel. It's fine if security has that information, but everyone in the hotel or venue should be invested in understanding what to do. Often, venues will not share their detailed emergency plans with you due to security reasons. However, they can still offer you guidelines on whom to contact, the chain of command, gathering spots, or other instructional direction so you can best guide your participants.

- Consult with your public safety professionals such as the local police, fire, and city agencies. Depending on the type of event, it is important to get their thoughts on your event, date, time, and overall impact on the community. For instance, perhaps you're planning a 5K race that will require shutting down streets, etc. You'll most likely need permits at the outset to even consider your event, but in terms of emergencies, law enforcement is your front-line partner in the chain of command and can provide invaluable insights and protections.

- Make sure you have the emergency contact information for all event participants. This is normally something captured during the registration phase. Equally important is to know the distance to your emergency facilities such as the hospital, fire department, police station, etc. It would also be helpful to know the back-up facilities that are nearby, for instance, if there's an overflow situation at a hospital.

It's important to always include planning for incidents as such, given the likelihood that they can happen. But, like the case study suggested, there are other emergencies and inconveniences that are important to manage as well.

Similar to conducting a needs assessment for external emergencies, at every stage of your planning process, you should be thinking about plan A, plan B, plan C, etc. This would include the venue, working with presenters/speakers, transportation issues, weather, printing materials, vendor issues, and other details related to your event. As you work through your timeline in pulling together the details, consider the following:

## Bucket Your Details into Categories

Bucket your details in categories such as Venue, Audio-Visual, Speakers, Printing, Production, Entertainment, Travel, and Amenities, among other relevant categories. The timelines that we produce at JDC Events normally are grouped as such and then further drilled down with relevant tasks under each category. By breaking down the categories and tasks, you can identify potential gaps. You should then use this format to note another column or section that specifically details "Contingencies." Think through every possible aspect that could go wrong, where you may need an alternative plan.

For instance, if you need to ship materials in advance, or you decide to bring select items with you that will be in checked luggage, what happens if your luggage is lost or the shipping company loses the packages? Perhaps there are master copies on a jump drive you can bring with you, or load them onto an internal cloud-based shared drive that can be downloaded to make additional copies as needed. This may not work in all situations, but the point is to think through each aspect and have a contingency plan. My company has had so many different things happen with every event that I could probably write another book just on that. But that's why it's so important to think through everything that you may not even think would be an issue. Take, for instance, something as simple as the lights going out in your meeting room because they are on the same circuit as another nearby room. You wouldn't normally think something like that would happen, but it did. And this was during a presentation. Or how about Super Bowl XLVII, where the lights went out for thirty-four minutes in the New Orleans Superdome? Since then, other Super Bowl stadiums have upgraded, inspected, backed up, and tested power systems months before the game.

It is also helpful for the event manager to meet with the key personnel involved in the process to develop these contingencies. It is equally valuable to discuss with your client (if applicable) or with your organization's key staff, vendors, and others as needed. This will lend additional intelligence on how to best respond. For larger events where you may have dignitaries, VIPs, and other notable guests, take this to another level with a special taskforce. However, whether large or small, it's important to start with each particular detail. Drill down from there to make sure you address any alternative needs should anything occur.

## Maintain an Updated Contacts List

With so many details in play, there will be many different people in the planning mix. It's important to know who does what, and when. For instance, at one of my client's events, we needed access to a room—but the point of contact wasn't answering any of her phones or other devices. While we asked the building support staff for help in opening the room, they needed approval from this particular person. Our main contact finally ended up responding, but when we had asked earlier in the planning phase if there was a backup, she'd indicated that she was the only person to manage everything onsite.

As you can probably conclude, this sort of arrangement is not functional or practical. That's why there are two pilots in the cockpit in case anything occurs. We probed further and found that our contact was *not* the only person with the authority to guide the building staff. Had we had this information prior, we would have placed that person's name on the list. Designing meetings and events often are more than just the logistics; they can involve territory protection, politics, and other factors that can impact your access to information. It's critical to gather multiple names for your planning categories who can serve as the point people for that detail. And revisit this list on a regular basis to ensure it remains as up-to-date as possible.

## Arrive Early

It never ceases to amaze me when event managers do not arrive early for their events. I have seen this on so many different occasions. The sooner you can get there, the better. This helps to fix any issues such as equipment that doesn't work or materials not arriving, wrong room sets, change in venue personnel, and other issues. This reminds me of a conference we held that involved transporting attendees to Capitol Hill to participate in an Advocacy Day event. The morning of the event, while participants were gathering in the lobby, we were notified that the transportation company had gone into receivership and would not be able to take participants to the Hill. We were also told not to board the shuttle if this same company showed up. So we executed our plan B by contacting another nearby company that could transport all participants. And, sure enough, the company in question did end up showing up, acting as if nothing had ever happened.

However, because we were there early, and had the time to make follow-up calls to the transportation company, we handled the situation in time. The participants may have had to wait a few extra minutes, but they were not aware of any issues. Arriving early—or even scheduling run-throughs in advance of your start time (if applicable)—is ideal in helping to mitigate any potential issues from the outset.

## Exhibit Grace Under Pressure

I have often been told that I am so "calm," and some are never quite sure if anything bothers me. Needless to say, there are many things that bother me; but when you are expected to be the leader in seeing details through to accomplish a goal, you simply just work through whatever issues are thrown at you and get it done. I've often seen high-strung event managers who wear their emotions on their sleeves. That's not a good characteristic for an event manager. If you are in a panic and acting crazy, you won't look confident in the overall experience. Think of when you're flying on a plane and you hit some turbulence. Often, I look at the flight attendants to see how they respond. If they're running up and down the aisle screaming, "We're all going to die!" that wouldn't make me feel very calm! However, when I see that they are calm, cool, and in control, just going around asking folks to double check their seatbelts and the like, that helps me not to be too worried—regardless that I don't enjoy the bumps.

When you exude confidence and control, many aspects that go wrong tend to go unnoticed. This will also help you address any areas that may need attention. At all of our events, we tend to roam the space while the event's in progress. This does a few different things. It allows you to ensure the details are properly executed, but it also alerts you to any potential issues. Perhaps you realize the meal service is somewhat slow when you notice the entire back of the room hasn't been served after a certain amount of time. You can then follow up with your banquet manager to determine if there's an issue. We ran into this not too long ago when the elevator used to transport meals to the hotel's main ballroom broke. It had apparently happened right before our event. So, we had to commission additional staff to get the meals to the room quicker. You might also hear people comment about the event elements; perhaps there was an unpleasant smell, or the food was a little cool...or many other things. But the point is, if you have your team constantly monitoring the event space for any issues, and then address them, nine times out of ten, you may not hear about them on an evaluation.

**Sharing is Caring**

In the business of managing events, being a micromanager or too controlling won't serve you well in meeting the event's goals and objectives. It's important for the event manager to be open and share all relevant information so everyone is on the same page in understanding their role. I mentioned earlier that the event manager should meet with the team and other key personnel involved in the process on a regular basis. While the event manager is responsible for the overall detail and outcomes, it's important that the other players understand their roles and the plan of action. Since they are to be involved from the start in identifying the contingency planning, they need to be kept up-to-date on the final plans—whether that's through meetings, work plan documents or another way of communicating. The point is to ensure everyone has access to and understands the protocol involving security, safety, and any other mishap that might occur. They should also be empowered to make their own decisions should it be necessary. So choosing the right team that can demonstrate good judgment and simply handle any situation is key.

The unexpected will be a regular factor in this field, which is why a strategy will generate a sense of calm and composure. You will never be able to provide a contingency plan for *every* issue, but you will be able to be ready through your personality and resolve in understanding it's your job to simply work through whatever situation arises. Strong problem-solving and decision- making skills will serve an event manager well in achieving greater success in uncertain times.

Having built transformative event experiences over the past twenty years, I know the power of events and how they can change individuals and organizations. That's why I've tried to offer you some insights as you embark on a journey to use this powerful communications tool. So I charge you to always think about whatever event you will create from the standpoint of the end users. What is it that you want them to walk away with; what do you want them to do different, learn, or feel? Much like what I discussed at the beginning of this book in defining the overall purpose, events are not about you. They are about delivering an important message that others can benefit from. Their power is enormous, and I wish you an exciting time in changing your communities—and ultimately the world—through impactful events.

# About the Author

Jennifer D. Collins, CMP, is the president and CEO of JDC Events—an award-winning event design company based in the Washington, D.C., area. Having started the business as the sole employee in a basement apartment in Washington, D.C., she is proud to have built a multimillion-dollar company that not only positions corporate, government and nonprofit clients to build stronger brands, but also changes the lives of their beneficiaries, whether by adopting new skills, learning new ideas that help others or participating in memorable experiences.

Because of Jennifer's leadership, the company has been ranked one of the top meeting and event companies in the Washington, D.C., region by the *Washington Business Journal* for multiple consecutive years. She also serves as a leader in the business community, including as a member of the Legacy Society of the Professional Convention Management Association (PCMA); vice chair of the Board of Directors for the Women Presidents' Educational Organization (WPEO); a member of the Women Presidents' Organization (WPO), a peer advisory group for women running multimillion-dollar companies; and a member of the Women's Enterprise Forum, an advisory group to the Women's Business Enterprise National Council (WBENC).

Always cognizant of paying it forward, Jennifer remains active with her alma mater, The American University, through guest lecturing; she's served on the Alumni Association Board and the School of Communications' Dean's Council, and committed a gift toward construction of the School of

Communications' first-ever building, where an office bears her name.

Jennifer has earned the coveted industry designation of Certified Meeting Professional (CMP); she graduated from The American University in Washington, D.C., and has attended the Tuck School of Business at Dartmouth Executive Education Program.

# About JDC Events

JDC Events is an event management and design company that positions corporate, nonprofit and government clients to build stronger brands through strategic events. Through strategic planning and creative logistical execution, our team builds engaging experiences that meet your organization's goals and objectives.

# Connect with the Author

**Website:**    www.jdc-events.com

**Email:**    info@jdc-events.com

**Social Media:**

**Facebook:**    www.facebook.com/jdceventsllc

**LinkedIn:**    https://www.linkedin.com/company/jdc-events-llc

98255901R00076

Made in the USA
Columbia, SC
21 June 2018